Front cover by Marilee B. Campbell
*The Lord's Harvest* Copyright © Marilee B. Campbell
All rights reserved

Self-Published on Amazon

First published in Great Britain 2020

ISBN: 9798684181214

# DEDICATION

This book is for those who wish to serve a full-time mission for the Church of Jesus Christ of Latter-day Saints and make a difference for yourself, your companion and the people that you will come across during this time.

These stories are taken directly from my and a few other missionaries' missions and I hope they will inspire you to prepare yourself for this unique opportunity to serve the Lord.

The central message of this book is that, if you but learn to connect with Heavenly Father and the Saviour, Jesus Christ, follow Their agenda and put full trust in Them, you will definitely gain an advantage as you will search, teach and baptise those who will be ready to accept the gospel. Of course, you will still need to exercise faith and work hard as this is your part of the deal.

Rest assured that They will keep Their part of the deal and bless your efforts according to your desires.

I know that you can make of this time the best time of your life, enriched with wonderful spiritual experiences and many opportunities to see the hand of the Lord manifested in your life and in the lives of those whose path you will come across. The rewards in terms of personal growth and connection with the divine will be unprecedented and will shape the rest of your life.

# ACKNOWLEDGEMENTS

Thanks to my parents who gave me life and supported me in my youth. I honour them along with my family who gave me encouragement and example through my youth and adulthood as I discovered my path and found my own way in life.

Thanks to my wife Imma, as this book would not have been possible without her encouragement and support, who has always been by my side during all these years of preparation.

Thanks also to my many teachers and mentors for sharing and helping to identify, verbalise and organise much of this material for this publication. We all must acknowledge that we can all give more than we get. We can be thankful for what we have and treat every person as though our life depended on them.

# TABLE OF CONTENTS

# PREFACE

Someone once said that we have 18 years to prepare to serve a mission, 2 years to live it and the rest of your life to think about it. As I reflect, I can easily see how this has been true for me.

Although I did not have 18 years to prepare, as I joined the Church one day before my eighteenth birthday, nevertheless I feel I lived my mission to the best of my mental, spiritual, and physical ability.

I still remember the neat feeling I got the very last evening in the mission field after returning home as I felt a pat on the shoulder from Heavenly Father saying, "I am happy with what you have done". I shall never forget it.

A few years ago, many years after I finished my mission, I came across a letter (enclosed at the end) that one of my companions had written to one of his friends who was then serving a full-time mission. In this letter he recounted some of the experiences we have had together as full-time missionaries.

Little did I know then that this letter had been passed around between missionaries around the world. Because of this distribution and the chance to connect via social media, I have been receiving numerous friendships requests on Facebook and emails from missionaries currently serving full-time missions or who have barely returned home.

I often felt humbled to know that missionaries were looking at me as a good example to follow. Missionaries seem to think that I am some kind of a superhero so they contact me asking how they can be bolder, help their companions be more committed, help their friends progress to baptism and how they can be guided by the Spirit.

I can see from their messages and questions that they are looking for help and guidance. They want to have success but sometimes they don't quite know what to do and how to do it.

So, for these reasons I am always very happy to chat with them and give some encouragement and words of advice. When I speak or chat with them, I always reinforce the idea that, as for ourselves, we can do nothing but that the Lord can make us mighty and guide us to His children who are ready to accept the gospel. As you can read in the letter I was, and still am very far from perfection, therefore no special powers unfortunately, but a lot of faith, hard work and trust that He can magnify our efforts exponentially.

Because of this interaction with missionaries around the world, I have recently come to the conclusion that perhaps I could share a few more experiences I have had and things I have learned whilst serving as a missionary of the Church of Jesus Christ of Latter-day Saints with the hope that they may be inspirational to help you embrace your missionary service with all your heart, might, mind and strength and become an instrument in Heavenly Father's hands to bring many of His children unto Christ.

# INTRODUCTION

As you are preparing to serve your mission you may be experiencing mixed feelings such as enthusiasm or indifference, courage or fear, faith or doubt. You may also be still trying to figure out whether it is worth leaving home for 18/24 months or maybe struggling to find the right motivation.

You may also be experiencing external pressure to leave or fear of disappointing your family and friends. You may also be excited and ready to serve but still wanting to know how you can be a successful missionary drawing upon the powers of heaven.

If you are already on a mission, you may be finding it hard to adjust to missionary life in general, or you may be struggling with finding a real purpose and motivation to go out every day and talk to strangers about the gospel.

Perhaps, you may not have a strong testimony yet, or you may have not yet come to terms with your fears and anxiety. If you are experiencing any of these feelings, I just want you to know that it's ok. Please don't lose hope in your potential and in what you can accomplish as a servant of the Lord.

Moroni taught, "And if men come unto me I will show unto them their weakness. I give unto men weakness that they may be humble; and my grace is sufficient for all men that humble themselves before me; for if they humble themselves before me, and have faith in me, then will I make weak things become strong unto them" (Ether 12:27).

I truly hope that by reading this book you will find, with the Lord's help, the power to make your weaknesses, whatever they may be, strong, find the right motivation and eliminate all the limiting assumptions that are preventing you from serving a mission or to make of it the best time of your life.

At the beginning of my mission I strongly believed that the Lord could help me to overcome my weaknesses and insecurities and that He could give me the courage to be a bold missionary. I learned through first-hand experience that He has the power to make us what we want to be and that He can make us as bold, as fearless, as powerful, and mighty as we want to be.

If you will trust Him enough, He will bless you with what you need to become a powerful instrument in His hands. Believe me, He did miracles with me. I am sure that He will do the same with you, too.

# CHAPTER 1

# UPBRINGING AND LIFE'S EARLY YEARS

*"For there are many yet on the earth among all sects, parties, and denominations, who are blinded by the subtle craftiness of men, whereby they lie in wait to deceive, and who are only kept from the truth because they know not where to find it" (D&C 123:12).*

I was born of goodly parents in a small town in Italy where I grew up and later joined the Church at age 17. I was raised as a Catholic with all that this entails. I attended mass every Sunday (including serving as an altar boy), I received all the ordinances such as infant baptism, Holy Communion, and Confirmation.

Before and during my early pre-teenage years I spent a lot of my free time at the local church oratory where I got involved and enjoyed all kinds of recreational and spiritual activities including catechism, gymnastics, and football. The oratory was a good environment for me, and I strongly believe that it represented for me and many young men and women a safe place to grow which kept me away from bad company and unwholesome habits.

I will be eternally grateful to my parents for giving me a Christian upbringing, which laid the foundation of my faith and prepared me for the time when I found the Lord's Church, the Church of Jesus Christ of Latter-day Saints.

When I joined the Church, I didn't have to change my life drastically as I was already living all the commandments apart from fasting and the law of tithing. However, although I always believed in God and Jesus Christ, I often felt a void regarding our purpose on earth and especially about life after death.

I remember reciting set prayers repeatedly without reaching out to my Father in Heaven in an effective way. I knew that God was there, but I didn't know how to communicate with Him. So, I kept looking for many years in the wrong direction until God finally showed me the way.

# CHAPTER 2

# MY CONVERSION

*"...As many of the Lamanites as believed in their preaching, and were converted unto the Lord, never did fall away" (Alma 23:6).*

If you haven't realised it by now, I am a convert to the Church. I was introduced to the gospel by a friend who invited me to attend a few Young Adult activities during the summer school break where I was able to make new friends who were members of the Church. Amongst these people, there was an American family that was living in my hometown at the time who was hosting a lot of these activities in their home.

Apart from mingling with members of the Church, what made the most impact was indeed the example set by this family. I mean, they weren't perfect, but I loved the unity and love that they felt and showed to each other. At the time there wasn't much love and unity in my home, so I desired to know what was making such a difference for them. Once I found out I could have tried to replicate that in my family.

As I soon figured out that this miraculous cure was the gospel of Jesus Christ, I began to investigate and to take the lessons from the missionaries to know more about it.

Nevertheless, although I was attracted to the Church, I wasn't particularly impressed with the message shared by the missionaries which I found frankly a little weird. As a matter of fact, I stopped speaking with the missionaries and going to church for a while.

However, after approximately a month, suddenly, one Sunday morning, I woke up with such a strong, clear, and overwhelming impression that I should go back to church, so much so that I couldn't resist it. I didn't know why, but it was clear to me that I had to go back. Suffice to say that, of course, that morning it all seemed so different, it all felt so true. No one had invited me back but the Lord Himself through the power of His Spirit.

My journey to becoming a member of the Church had just begun. Soon after I began to speak again with the missionaries, I felt the desire that my parents, whom I loved dearly, might listen too. My ultimate desire then was that, through the gospel in our lives, we could experience, like my American friends, reciprocal feelings of love, respect and unity in our home.

To make a long story short, we all got baptised one day before my eighteenth birthday. I am sure you are now wondering whether the gospel produced the changes that I was looking for in my family or not. The answer is an absolute yes. Things changed drastically for the better for all of us and we were, finally, able to live in peace and reciprocal love.

Since my early days in the Church I was able to witness the great power found in the gospel of Jesus Christ, the power to change people and their lives for the better.

What is the status of your conversion? Do you feel you are converted? I believe these are questions you should ask yourself before you embark in such great work. The Lord said to His disciples "…and when thou art converted strengthen thy brethren" (Luke 22:32). This statement teaches us to be in the position to strengthen others and it is critical that we first assimilate the gospel's teaching in our lives and that we apply them to our behaviour.

Although conversion is a lifetime process and you don't have to be fully converted to serve a mission, at least you need to build a strong enough foundation to kindle that fire which will allow you to strengthen and empower those you will come across during your mission. The reason why I am sharing my upbringing and conversion story with you is to emphasise the importance of your preparation to serve the Lord as one of His special missionaries.

You know there can be many reasons to serve a mission. Perhaps your girlfriend would marry only a returned missionary or you want to go because all your friends are going. Maybe you want to go because this is your family's expectation, or you want to avoid the shame being the only one who hasn't gone.

If you decide to serve a mission for one of these or similar reasons, be prepared to come to terms with it sooner or later during your mission. So, please seek for the right reason to serve the Lord as a missionary, seek to obtain the word and a vision of the great work of salvation. Seek to develop a personal relationship with the Saviour and let Him change your heart and become converted to His gospel.

If you are feeling great and have the right motivation and purpose to serve the Lord as a missionary, then that's wonderful. Make sure you continue to feed your good feelings as this will be an advantage for you once you hit the road in the mission field.

When the sons of Mosiah were converted and felt God's love, they immediately wanted others to feel it too! That is why they decided to serve a mission for fourteen years amongst their worst enemies. They didn't go on holiday or for an away football game, they went so that somehow, they could be the means to bring some of them "...to the knowledge of the of the Lord their God" (Mosiah 28:2).

For me there was no preparation through Primary, Seminary, the Young Men's Program and the Aaronic Priesthood so I didn't have the chance to grow my testimony gradually until it was strong enough to want to share it.

However, the Lord prepared me in another way and through different experiences which led to my conversion at the right time of my life. When the Lord called, I was ready because my heart was prepared to say, "Yes, Lord I will follow and serve Thee with all my might, mind and strength".

One of the ways that the Lord prepared me was through the service He called me to before I served my mission. I remember, particularly, when I received the calling to serve as a member of the district high council just after I turned 19.

As the youngest member of the council I was assigned to visit the Rimini Branch, a church unit situated on the east side of Italy by the Adriatic Sea. Now, considering that I lived on the opposite side of Italy I soon realised that my journey was going to be awfully long should I decide to visit this branch.

However, despite the distance and with all the enthusiasm possible for 19-year-old young man I began to plan my trip to visit the saints in that city. I soon realised that the trip would be longer than I thought. Nevertheless, I made up my mind and indeed visited the saints in Rimini.

At this point, I think you would be interested to know what was so unique about this trip. First, I had to take three trains through the night to be there on time for church in the morning and, second, I had to leave at 11:00 p.m. the day before to be able to arrive at 8:30 a.m. the following morning.

I remember that trip very well. How could I forget? It was cold, it was boring, and it was long. After giving my talk and training to the local members, I approached my return trip with renewed enthusiasm and strength only to realise, again very soon, that my journey back would be as cold and as boring as the previous night's one. I arrived exhausted back home around midnight and fell asleep in my bed straightaway.

For many years, I asked myself why on earth my District President had sent me so far away. He would often say, "You have to find out by yourself".

It took me quite a while to figure out the answer. Eventually, I came to the conclusion that the Lord wanted to teach me was the importance of sacrifice and putting Him first, however difficult the circumstances might be. He wanted to teach me to go and do what He commands even by the voice of His servants and to be faithful in doing His will no matter what.

This important lesson represented for me my spiritual crossroads. To this day, it still has a tremendous and critical impact on my attitude in all that I do.

I hope that you can seriously consider preparing yourself to represent the Saviour in this marvellous work of spreading the good news so that you will be able to be used as a powerful instrument in His hands to touch people's hearts and help them to come unto Christ.

Just think for a moment: what can I do to be a worthier recipient of His help and guidance? What can I do to be more in tune with the Spirit and draw upon the powers of heaven? I am telling you this because worthiness and the

16

companionship of the Holy Ghost are fundamental in qualifying you to draw upon the powers of heaven, enabling you to use them both during your service as a missionary and for the rest of your life.

If there is anything that you feel you need to repent of, please go now to your bishop and start the repentance process. Everything can be worked out and the Lord truly forgives us when we repent.

The sons of Mosiah and Alma the Younger felt they were the "the very vilest of sinners" (Mosiah 28:4), but the Lord was merciful towards them. They repented and became relentless missionaries.

Nobody is perfect and we all make mistakes, but Heavenly Father always gives us another chance. I am sure they all learned a lot from their mistakes, and feeling the redeeming love of the Saviour made them different men. It was indeed this transformation of their weaknesses into strengths and the change of their hearts that made them into the powerful missionaries they became.

As President Hinckley said: "Live worthy of a call and respond without hesitation when that call comes. Go forth with a spirit of dedication, placing yourself in the hands of the Lord to do His great work."

# CHAPTER 3

# THE POWER OF YOUR TESTIMONY

*"But the Comforter, which is the Holy Ghost, whom the Father will send in my name, he shall teach you all things, and bring all things to your remembrance, whatsoever I have said unto you" (John 14:26).*

When I listen to opera singers, I can't help but marvel at what they can accomplish with their voices in terms of power and sound. They seem to be able to penetrate deeply in my heart and touch the invisible chords of my soul.

From the time I was a missionary until today, I strongly believed that the Spirit can place my testimony in the hearts of those with whom I share, just as an opera singer can trigger an emotion in my soul.

There were many occasions when I witnessed the miracle that occurs when we open our mouths to bear testimony of the truthfulness of the gospel of Jesus Christ. I still remember as if it was now, how the Spirit touched the people I taught about the prophet Joseph Smith.

Each time I bore testimony of the First Vision I walked in the sacred grove with the people I was teaching. The Spirit seemed to permeate the atmosphere in those rooms, and it was impossible not to feel it. At this point, the only thing I could do was to help the person recognise where this feeling was coming from and it was job done; the Spirit had sealed my words into their hearts.

Before I joined the Church however, my testimony was just like a little plant, with great potential but still fragile and unstable. It needed strengthening, watering and a lot of care and nourishment.

The Lord had placed a portion of the word in my heart and mind and had burned it down in my soul by His Spirit but it was now up to me to grow it and make it stronger and stronger. When I received my mission call, my testimony was not that strong yet.

Yes, I believed that the Church had been restored, that The Book of Mormon contained the word of God and that Joseph Smith was called as a prophet, but I didn't know it for myself. I decided that I couldn't spend two years of my life going around teaching people about something I did not know for myself.

So, I committed myself to make the attempt to obtain this testimony and I began to read The Book of Mormon from start to end. Then one day, although I don't recall exactly what and where I was reading, the Spirit of the Lord took over me to confirm that the book was true.

I still remember the wonderful feeling that embraced me. It filled every fibre of my body so that I was overpowered by this burning in my bosom. I knew now for myself. Great joy came into my heart. I was now ready to go forth and share my testimony with the people of England.

I am aware that for those of you who grew up in the Church, perhaps your testimony has not come in such an overwhelmingly physical way but much more gradually until it became as strong, indicative and persuasive of true conversion as mine.

What I am trying to say is that it is important that, no matter how you received it, it's important that you begin your mission with a sure testimony of the things you are going to teach. If you don't have a testimony of your own, how can you think that you can touch other people's hearts?

If you were a salesman you would have to believe 100% that whatever product you are selling is indeed a good product to buy, otherwise, how do you think that the people you are trying to sell it to would be convinced?

I am not saying that you must have a testimony as strong as Alma the Younger and the sons of Mosiah. I didn't either by the way. Nonetheless, you should have a strong enough testimony for yourself, and to touch the people you teach. In other words, it shouldn't be as small as a seed like in Alma's sermon, not yet sprouted. It should at least be like a stable plant that will continue to grow gradually into a strong big tree as you nourish it through study, prayer and by serving others.

# CHAPTER 4

# BE UNSTOPPABLE

*"And it came to pass that I, Nephi, said unto my father: I will go and do the things which the Lord hath commanded, for I know that the Lord giveth no commandments unto the children of men, save he shall prepare a way for them that they may accomplish the thing which he commandeth them" (1 Nephi 3:7).*

My first experience as a missionary of the Church of Jesus Christ of Latter-day Saints in England wasn't a very interesting one. However, it was certainly one that I shall never forget.

When I arrived at Heathrow Airport, I was supposed to be picked up by the MTC missionaries, but unexpectedly no one showed up. "What on earth am I going to do now?" I thought to myself! I can't speak English well and I don't have a clue about where I need to go. Pretty good start, right?

When I was about to sink into despair, I partially overheard an announcement mentioning the Church that said to go to a certain place in the airport. I thought, "I am saved". Unfortunately, when I got to this meeting point, instead of finding the people who were supposed to pick me up I found another sister missionary from Spain who was looking for help, too. I thought, "Oh boy, now what?" The scenario appeared to be even worse than before. I couldn't speak Spanish, she couldn't speak Italian and neither of us could speak English. Indeed, we were in serious trouble!

Time was running out and we didn't have a solution. Then I felt inspired to look for the number of the London Mission and I called them with my broken English to ask for help and directions.

I still don't know how I managed to talk to them over the phone, but I soon realised that no one was going to pick us up. I thought, "This is definitely not a good start!" With difficulty I tried to understand how we could make our way to the MTC, which was some distance from London. The journey required us to take several trains and buses, and finally a taxi.

Besides this, the sister missionary had a ton of luggage with her (she must have brought the entire bedroom with her!). So, I had to carry a few of her suitcases plus mine through London, via Victoria Station to Lingfield and the MTC.

If I think about it now, I honestly don't know how we got there as I don't remember the journey at all. When I arrived at the MTC I was still very much troubled with many conflicting thoughts.

Although I knew that I was doing the right thing, I began to question my very presence in a foreign country away from home. I believe that the adversary was certainly trying to weaken my spiritual defences and put me off.

I thought, "What if my parents were right? What if I am wasting my time? What if they sell the business? What will I do after my mission?" I also struggled quite a bit at the beginning with the language which didn't help me at all to feel better.

I can honestly say that my three weeks at the MTC didn't turn out to be the best of my life. However, I didn't let despair and anxiety overpower me and I pushed through trying to learn as much as I could and to improve my language skills.

My determination to learn the language as well as the gift of tongues with which I was blessed, certainly, played a critical role in my quick adjustment and full integration into missionary life.

I committed myself to study regularly and to strive to learn new words and gain more confidence every day. I trusted that the Lord would fill the gap. As matter of fact, I became very fluent in English, just before the six months' mark.

Nothing could deter me from doing what I was supposed to be doing. I still vividly remember an experience I had with the gift of tongues during the early part of my mission in one of the first teaching appointments I had ever been in.

We were teaching the plan of salvation and, of course, my companion was taking the lead as I still wasn't extremely comfortable with English. I mean, I knew the contents of the discussions, but I couldn't express myself very well.

What happened in the middle of the discussion was something that left me and my companion stunned. As soon as he got over teaching one section of the discussion I unexpectedly took over and taught in perfect English the next one without hesitation. I felt so confident that I could deliver this part of the discussion, it didn't even cross my mind then that anything would go wrong.

As I finished teaching, I looked at my companion like nothing had happened only to realise that he was looking at me as his jaw dropped in surprise. I quickly realised what had just happened and marvelled at the power of the Spirit enabling me to teach.

As we left these people's homes, we continued to talk about this wonderful manifestation of the Spirit, especially as we realised that I returned to my previous speaking level right after I taught.

To further illustrate the importance of becoming unstoppable no matter what, I shall share a trial of my faith I experienced when I was at about two thirds of the way through my mission. For some reason and without any warning, I stopped receiving money from my district back home.

So, the immediate result was that I ran out of money quite quickly, and was left wondering what I could do now.

At first, I trusted that all could be sorted out quite soon. But unfortunately, I soon realised that situation would go on for some time. No matter what I did, telephone calls or letters, nothing happened.

At this point I can't say that I had the best feelings for the leaders back home. How could they do this to me? How could they be so careless?

Feelings of anger and resentment began to creep up and I felt that my service as a missionary would inevitably be thwarted.

As I prayed for comfort in this difficult situation, I believe that I was blessed with extra strength and resilience in order to cope. Even my negative thoughts about people and the situation itself seemed to fade away. So, I accepted the circumstances and I continued to work as hard as I could.

You may now wonder how I survived without much food for a few months. The answer is that I managed to live on boiled potatoes for quite a few weeks because it was the only food I could afford. In other words, potatoes for breakfast, lunch, and dinner

And this wasn't all. To be unified, my companion applied the same diet to himself and the other missionaries in the district cooked for us quite a few times.

On top of this, out of nowhere, a friend from home sent me some money, I wasn't expecting at all. He later told me that he had received a prompting from the Spirit to send me the money without knowing the situation.

This experience reminded me of the words of the Saviour when he said, "Therefore I say unto you, Take no thought for your life, what ye shall eat, or what ye shall drink; nor yet for your body, what ye shall put on. Is not the life more than meat, and the body than raiment? Behold the fowls of the air, for they sow not, neither do they reap, nor gather into barns; yet your heavenly Father feedeth them. Are ye not much better than they?" (Matthew 6:25-26).

Indeed, I was more than the fowls of the air and the Lord had provided for me without sowing, reaping or gathering into barns.

Eventually I started to receive money again as I have said, and after a couple of months, I was able to restore a stable financial situation.

What I am trying to say is that there will be many times during your service as a missionary when you will find obstacles along your way. The adversary will undoubtedly try to influence you negatively, to put you off course.

Perhaps, you will struggle with some of your companions' attitude toward the work or their peculiar personality. Why not? Most probably you will face general opposition in the form of tests of your faith and endurance that you can't predict at this stage. I am not trying to scare you off because you don't have to fear anything being on the Lord's side. However, you need to be prepared and consider that it won't be a walk in the park.

No matter what happens you should never give up. No matter how difficult or unfair things may be, you must resiliently push forward and wait for the hand of the Lord to be manifested.

Just remember that you won't be forgotten, and as the fowls of the air, the Lord will remember you and look after you and administer to your needs.

I know for a surety that His hand will be manifested many times during your mission, and that you will see miracles as you push yourself out of your comfort zone to reach the magic zone where miracles happen in your life and in the lives of those whom you serve. I know it because I have seen it.

# CHAPTER 5

# YOU HAVE WORK TO DO

*"Now behold, a marvelous work is about to come forth among the children of men" (D&C 4:1.)*

My first interview with my Mission President was something that has been in my heart since that moment. I occasionally reflect on this experience when I feel inspired. He was a very gentle and yet powerful man who put me at ease straightaway. He realised that I couldn't speak English that well. He was the kind of person who could see right through you, but his gaze was at the same time sweet and gentle. I felt safe and in good hands.

We talked at first about the usual things such as my background, my family and of course about my mission. He asked me what kind of a missionary I wanted to be and if I had any goals. That question, "What kind of a missionary do I want to be?" sunk deep into my heart and mind, so much so that right there and then I felt strongly to commit to becoming the best missionary I could be and to work hard every single hour for the next two years.

As the interview was ending, he paused for a minute and shared an impression he had about my future. He said, "Elder I don't know why I am feeling this, but I feel constrained by the Spirit to tell you that the Lord will call you to do something special in your country. I don't know what it will be, but I know that it will be special."

As soon as he pronounced these words, I felt struck by the Spirit bearing testimony to the innermost part of my soul that what I had just heard was true. We closed the interview and we left the room to join the other group of missionaries who were waiting to be assigned to a companion.

The reason why I am sharing such a personal experience is to bear witness of the Holy Ghost's inspiration to guide us to know what Heavenly Father expects from us.

A few weeks later, after this interview, I became determined to receive my patriarchal blessing. I was still pondering my Mission President's words and I wanted to know more about it.

The reason why I hadn't received my patriarchal blessing yet, was because in Italy at that time we didn't have stakes, so the only chance to receive it was when a patriarch was sent from another country. I missed the only opportunity that arose because he came as I was away for my civil service training as a fire-fighter. Anyway, to make a long story short, I went to a stake patriarch ready to receive guidance from the Lord.

We usually don't share publicly what is in our patriarchal blessings. It suffices to say that he delivered the same message, but with more information than my mission president had previously shared. I couldn't believe it. It was indeed true!

In the years after my mission, I saw all these prophecies regarding myself gradually come to pass, as I have had opportunities to serve that enabled me to see the Church grow and develop in my own country. My mind has gone back often to the words of my mission president, and each time that I served they resonated with me just like they did over thirty years ago.

So dear friend, you also have work to do. You and only you can do what you can do. Every one of us is unique and we all have a different purpose which we are blessed to come to know through inspiring leaders, our patriarchal blessing or through our service.

You, as a missionary, are meant to leave a mark in this world and with the people you will meet during your journey as a servant of the Lord. It is indeed a great responsibility, but you aren't on your own.

Don't forget that you are working shoulder to shoulder with Heavenly Father and His Son Jesus Christ. What could you ever be afraid of in such company? You are bound to succeed, just seek a vision of what the Lord is calling you to do and then give it your absolute best shot.

The reward is unimaginable for you and for those whom you will find during your search for the elect: happiness in this life and in the life to come. Shall you not be thoroughly engaged in such a great cause?

# CHAPTER 6

# BE ONE

*"...If you are not one you are not mine" (D&C 38:27).*

I loved and appreciated all my companions, I learned from all of them and I am thankful for the time we spent together. Yet my challenge during my mission was to work with those of them who, perhaps, didn't share the same enthusiasm and desire to work as hard as I wanted to.

I am sure that I also had many limitations, but this feeling of always being in a hurry to speak with as many people as possible, at times clashed with a more relaxed way of doing missionary work favoured by some other missionaries.

You know, I just felt that I didn't want to waste a minute of my time. So, I was a pushy companion, in the sense that I was always pushing to do more, push, push and push! I wouldn't stop in front of anyone including my companions and anything else that might get in my way.

I remember one time I was in the car with another missionary during a very cold and snowy day. While I thought that we were getting to go out, he mentioned that he wanted to stay in the car to enjoy the warmth and, perhaps, rest for a while. I was flabbergasted!

"What do you mean we are staying in the car? For how long?" I knew that I couldn't leave my companion alone in the car so what could I do? Could I just take a nap, too? Of course not!

One option was to stay inside the car and read the scriptures, but my never-ending motivational engine wouldn't stop, insisting that I "Get out, get out!" As I was praying to the Lord for inspiration to find a way to do missionary work without leaving the other missionary alone, I felt inspired to get out of the car, lock it, and begin speaking with people who were walking close enough to enable me to maintain an eye on him.

If anyone asked me about the other missionary in the car, I replied that he wasn't well and needed a rest. I also told them that I couldn't bear to stay in the car, because I had the best message in the world to share with them'

Thankfully, he didn't sleep for too long and we were able to resume missionary work together quite soon.

Much wrestling went on with the Lord and many tears were shed before I realised that my companions were the first people I was responsible for, and that I had to seek unity and cohesion instead of pressing forward without considering their feelings or struggles. No matter how many people I helped to find their way to the Church, if I failed with each of my companions, I would have failed all the way.

Jesus cared for His disciples. He helped them overcome their weaknesses and he forgave them, encouraged them, and helped them achieve their highest potential. I had to follow His example.

As a manner of fact, during the second part of my mission I became less pushy and more tolerant. The words of the Saviour "If you are not one you are not mine" resonated with me so much, that they became ingrained in my new approach to missionary work. I took more time to understand what my companions were going through and to work at their pace.

Certainly, my idea was always the same, work hard and to speak with as many people as possible. Nevertheless, I opted for a more united effort at a little slower pace, which turned out to be highly effective anyway. I can honestly say that the results we obtained when we worked in a unified way were the same as when I felt as though I was dragging my companions around. We were able to find, speak with and baptise just as many people.

One of the most successful stories that I can remember is about my relationship with one of my companions. I will call him Elder White.

Elder White was a nice guy. He liked joking around a lot and had a strong interest in wrestling. As a manner of fact, he wanted to wrestle me all the time. Sometimes I succeeded avoiding physical contact, but at times I had to defend myself when he ambushed me from behind a door or closet. He was a great eater, too, so much so that he wouldn't only eat the food on his plate but from mine, too. He got on my nerves quite often and at times I thought I was dealing with a child. However, I tried my best to be patient and to avoid showing my discomfort openly. I sought to look at him as the Saviour would, and in time, I learned to love him dearly despite his peculiar habits and we got on quite well.

During our time together, after I decided to focus on my companion's potential rather than on the things that irritated me, he responded positively by developing his strengths as a missionary. Eventually, a member of the ward we were serving in approached me and said, "Since you have been with Elder White, he has become a much better missionary.' Nothing could have sounded more beautiful to me, and although I can't take any credit for his improvement, I think that my decision to love him better was a key element in helping him to change. I'm quite sure that as he felt accepted and loved, he naturally desired to be better and do better.'

When I think about missionary companionship, I always remember the example of Alma and Amulek. We could imagine that God was the mission president. He assigned Alma to work with Amulek, a not very active member at the time. However, God knew Amulek's potential very well so he paired him up with Alma hoping that he could help him to become the best version of himself.

After they finally met, Alma spent quite a bit of time patiently training Amulek who later became very valiant in testimony and desired to follow Alma becoming a powerful missionary. The rest is history. We all know what happened.

So, please take good care of your companions. If they don't have the same motivation, strength or desire that you have, perhaps slow down a little and let them catch up with you in a spirit of love and tolerance. Seek to become one, just as the Saviour revealed to the Prophet Joseph Smith when He said, "If ye are not one ye are not mine" (D&C 38:27).

This work isn't a competitive race and, although it's very urgent, you can't leave people behind, including your companion. The harvest will be abundant when you work together.

Remember that Heavenly Father wants you, as a companionship, to be successful, to learn from each other and grow together. He is there to help you if you seek His guidance. You can pray and ask Heavenly Father how you can help a difficult companion, how you can learn to get on and love them despite their faults.

Nobody is perfect including me and you, but we are all worthy of love. Let's learn to see others with Heavenly Father's eyes, and this will help us to be more tolerant and more loving. Love can make miracles!

# CHAPTER 7

# WORK HARD

*"Therefore, O ye that embark in the service of God, see that ye serve him with all your heart, might, mind and strength..." (Mosiah 4:2).*

Apparently, at transfer time Elders hoped that they wouldn't be paired up with me. I was nicknamed "the workhorse". I don't know how this nickname came about or who created it but indeed some missionaries confessed that they would have preferred not to be transferred with me due to my fame of working really hard.

Although I didn't know if I should take it as a compliment or more as a negative label, I kind of liked the idea and the reputation. As a matter of fact, that is exactly what I had signed up for at the beginning of my mission. I wanted to be the best missionary that I could be and to speak with as many people as I could without wasting time.

For sure, this is what I did throughout my mission. I never held back or was tentative in finding, teaching, and baptising those of Heavenly Father's children who were ready to accept the gospel.

As I knew that my time as a missionary wouldn't last forever, I was super determined to make the most effective use of it. This feeling of urgency accompanied me during my entire mission, and when my time as a missionary was over, I was blessed to be able to extend for an additional month and was afforded a little bit more time to continue to serve the Lord.

The following story is a good example of this burning desire. Two months before the end of my mission, I received a call from the mission president who called me to train a new missionary and to open a new area. I was assigned as a district leader in a district that included two other sets of missionaries, two elders and two sisters. The sisters had a car and we and the other elders were on bikes which was a perceived injustice. Besides this, we had to ride our bikes across hills for an hour to get into our proselyting area.

I took this challenge with all my heart and I set off to work with my new companion. Considering that I was almost at the end of my mission, I thought the only one way to remain focused until the end was to withhold from my companion and the members that I was going home in two months. I don't know how I managed to keep the secret, but it worked out really well until the end. As a matter of fact, my companion and I worked really hard through those two months, so I was able to stay focused on the work, hopefully provide good leadership to the other missionaries and speak with as many people as possible.

I still remember very vividly my last day in the field. As usual, we rose early and then had companion study and personal study. Also, as usual, I ironed my companion's shirt. We were ready to go out on time.

My last day had to be no different than any other day during my mission. I asked my companion if it was okay to go the extra mile that day which he cheerfully agreed to. I remember that in the evening we went to tract in a residential area where we found a nice family who let us in so we could teach them.

We taught a good discussion and we obtained an appointment to come back. That was it. It was now 9:30

pm, time to go home. On our way home my companion was excited for the family we had found and eventually he asked me for our plan the next day. The time to reveal the secret had arrived.

I stopped in front of our door and said, "Elder there is not going to be a tomorrow for me."

He then looked at me puzzled and exclaimed, "What do you mean, Elder?"

"I am going home, Elder, I am done!"

"Going home?"

"Yes, I am going home."

That night as I finally packed my belongings, I was overwhelmed by such a beautiful feeling as I had never experienced before. The Lord was pleased with my offering, I had raced well, I had fought a good fight. I was confident that I had done all that I could, never holding back.

One of the rules on my mission as a trainer was to wake up an hour early each morning to have more time to study, especially for those new missionaries who were learning a new language. Of course, I woke up every morning at 5:30 as a new missionary (greeny) and when I trained, but I did also with all my other companions for my entire mission. I thought that having some extra time would have given me more time to study individually and to plan better for the day ahead. And it did!

As none of my companions agreed to do this except for my trainer and the new missionaries that I trained, I pretty much carried on waking up earlier on my own. I was particularly very keen to study The Book of Mormon, especially the stories about the great missionaries of the time such as Ammon or Alma. I felt that if they had obtained so much success why couldn't I? There was only one way to acquire the power to convince others, and that was to understand the Lord's word so that I could then teach and testify with power, and help people act on the desire to change.

I witnessed many times how the Lord can use us as an instrument to bless His children's lives. I know that if you, too, will study hard to understand His words, you can receive power to convince others, and you will see many doors opened and many hearts converted.

If you knew that this power was real and that you could obtain it, what difference would it make in your missionary efforts? What can you do now to obtain the power to the convincing of men?

# CHAPTER 8

# THE EXTRA MILE

*"And whosoever shall compel thee to go a mile, go with him twain" (3 Nephi 12:41).*

One of my strong beliefs as a young man was that my car could run indefinitely with little fuel. I used to fill the tank partially and then assume that I could use my car with that fuel forever. My firm belief was that my car could always go the extra mile! Now, I don't know if it was faith or that I believed in miracles, but it suffices to say that, to my great disappointment, my car let me down and stopped in the middle of the road quite a few times. After having pushed the car multiple times, I finally learned that my belief had no foundation whatsoever.

As a new missionary I still hadn't learned what going the extra mile was really about. I remember that my companion and I were fasting, although I don't quite recall the reason or if it was for the usual fast that we do during the first Sunday of each month. I remember once when my companion and I were fasting on a very hot Sunday during the summer. After church we decided to keep fasting forward and find people to teach in the afternoon.

Now you can easily imagine what it was like to be fasting for such a long time, especially during one of the hottest days I can ever remember during my mission. My mouth was as dry as the Sahara Desert, my legs felt as wobbly as a piece of jelly and my jaw was constantly dropped so that I could not even speak. We figured out that we had made a very silly decision and therefore we headed immediately back home.

We certainly hadn't been very wise. The words of King Benjamin resonated with us for a while, "...for it is not requisite that, a man should run faster than he has strength" and that, "...all things must be done in order" (Mosiah 4:27).

So, what does it mean to go the extra mile?

I recently spoke with one of my companions who shared with me an episode he recalled when we were doing some finding by knocking on doors. He said, "My friend I clearly remember that, 'as new missionary I had had enough of knocking on doors, but you kept going saying, 'C'mon, let's do one more, perhaps the next will be the right one'. The problem was that we didn't just knock on only one more door, but we kept going for quite a while, and you kept repeating the same slogan over and over again".

Now this story isn't that big of a deal. (I don't even remember if we got in or found anyone) However, it's a good example to illustrate my point, which is, that going the extra mile means that you are willing to make a special effort to do or achieve something. It is only when you are willing to exert that extra effort, to work that extra hour, to speak with that extra person, to knock on that extra door, that you have access to the powers of heaven.

If you look at the scriptures, you can find many examples of missionaries who went the extra mile and achieved great things. The sons of Mosiah spent fourteen years amongst the Lamanites trying to bring them to the knowledge of their Redeemer. Now, I don't know what the rules were in terms of mission timings, but I am sure that you agree with me, that what they did went beyond normal duty.

Take Ammon, for example. His responsibility was to

teach the Lamanites, but as he entered the land of Ishmael he was immediately taken and brought before King Lamoni. When asked about his purpose for being there, Ammon replied that he wanted to dwell there and be the King's servant. Now, he did not start preaching to the King straightaway but offered his service. He even went further watching over the King's flock and defending it from some band of robbers.

It's clear to me that Ammon went the extra mile. He went beyond his duty and responsibility. Because of this, he was able to access the powers of Heaven and literally bring hundreds to the knowledge of the Lord, their Redeemer. Can you see where I am coming from?

When I was serving in Birmingham, we met a nice couple who were willing to listen to us. They were good people and we loved them dearly. Before we even began to teach them, we offered our service as part of our sincere interest and love for them. However, the task proved to be more daunting that we thought. At first, we thought that we had to strip the wallpaper from just one room, but we soon realised that we had to strip all the wallpaper in the flat. Now, I wasn't then, and I am still not, a lover of wallpaper stripping, but we took the chance to serve them this way. We spent the entire day stripping wallpaper, and this gave us many opportunities to share in a natural way many things about the gospel of Jesus Christ. Well, to make a long story short this couple continued to receive discussions and was eventually baptised.

Service is definitely a wonderful way to go the extra mile by showing sincere love, which in turn touches people's hearts and prepares them to accept your message.

A while ago, I happened to eat some cheese and an apple together. As I did this, my mind went back to my mission and I remembered that Cheddar cheese and an apple was for a while my preferred lunch.

I don't know if you have tried it, but the sweetness and crispy texture of the apple together with the softness and strong flavour of the Cheddar cheese, makes a delicious and refreshing lunch. Anyway, I am not interested to provide easy and quick recipes for your lunches. What I want to tell you is about why we ate quick and simple lunches for a while during my mission.

As missionaries, we soon realised that the best time of the day to find people in the streets was the lunch break. What shall we do? we wondered! We figured out that the only way to use our time productively was to give up a large chunk of our lunch. The only way to do that was to have a quick and simple lunch. What shall we do? we thought. Then we remembered that the Mission President's wife had suggested an extremely healthy and simple lunch, apple and cheese. We had found the solution. From that point on, we had apple and cheese every day for lunch and by so doing we were able to use this time to find people in the town centre.

I still remember the wonderful experiences that we were blessed with during those lunch breaks. We felt that we were endowed by special powers to discern who was keener to listen to us and accept a commitment. I remember that, on more than one occasion, I felt strongly that I should speak with a person who was walking by whilst I was speaking with someone else. It was a strange feeling, as I was being pulled out of that conversation in order to stop that person that was walking past. Probably the best way to describe it is that it was like an extraordinarily strong prompting. I had to speak with that person. I still don't quite understand how it worked, but it was a real thing and it was quite clear to me that it was coming from the Holy Ghost.

Sometimes I even ran to chase the person before she/he disappeared from my sight. My approach was straightforward, "Hi, I am a missionary of the Church of Jesus Christ of Latter-day Saints. I am sorry to bother you, but I just felt strongly that I should talk to you!" Now, I honestly say that sometimes some of those people didn't turn out to be willing to accept an appointment, but some of them were actually people who were looking for something in their life.

What I want to say is that if you want to enter miraculous territory and have access to the powers of Heaven, you have to be willing to go the extra mile, to exert that extra effort that will align you, and help you attune with the Spirit of the Lord and bless you with unique guidance and inspiration.

This was certainly the case of Elder Cunia who was serving as assistant to the mission president at the beginning of my mission. This is his story in his own words.

"The days before the series of zone conferences at the beginning of November 1985 were intense. Elder Astle, the new assistant to the mission president, was to be trained by me. Zone conferences were to be prepared, transfers of more than 200 missionaries to be planned out and decided upon, interviews with new zone and district leaders as well as trainers to be planned and conducted, training material to be created and all that amidst the whirlwind of our daily business. Oh yes, Christmas conferences were to be prepared, venues to be evaluated, visited and finally chosen. The days were truly long and the nights short, hardly ever more than five hours of sleep. I had got my hands full to supervise these activities. Time and time again I wanted to prepare my own workshop for the upcoming series of zone conferences. For the benefit

42

of those who needed my help I postponed my preparations from one day to another.

"The final day before the first zone conference we managed to finish our preparations late in the evening. Everything was ready – except for my own workshop. We would need to get up at 4 am to pick up President and Sister Nielson and drive up to Newcastle for the first zone conference. At 10 pm I finally wanted to begin preparing my workshop as the other two missionaries in our flat started with a disagreement that soon developed to an unbearable extent. They came to see Elder Astle and me and asked for mediation. So, we supported them in clearing the situation. They were very thankful after our conversation of more than two hours. At 1 am I was able to commence the preparation of my workshop.

"I was not only physically drained; I did not have anything to teach the missionaries the next morning (actually the same morning). I sank to my knees and pleaded with the Lord: 'I have done all I could to prepare the upcoming events. I have trained Elder Astle, my new companion. From this time onward he will be able to do great by himself. I have taken care of all individuals and the entire mission. In a few hours the Elders and Sisters of this mission will await my spiritual input on how they should go about their work. From a year and a half of experience I could easily come up with something just like that. But this is not what I want. I do not want the missionaries to hear something from me. I want them to hear from Thee. It is Thy work. I want to be the one who conveys Thy will to them. Please tell me what to teach.' I concluded my pleadings and began to hear a voice, 'This is what you should teach them.' Then this voice spoke to me for a whole hour. It was clear and distinct as if a person sat directly beside me. I began to write what I had heard verbatim. A full page was soon filled, another one quickly followed. I heard scriptures indicated between the dictated pages. Many of these scriptures I knew and thought they were great at the respective passages. Some scriptures I did not know and wanted to look them up, but the voice continued to speak, and I struggled to keep up writing. After exactly one hour the voice stopped dictating. The workshop was completed. Although I was dog-tired, I was wide awake. After pondering over this matchless experience for a while, I asked myself whether Joseph Smith had received his revelations in a similar way. Then I fell asleep.

"Two hours later, I dragged myself out of bed. Elder Astle and I got on our way to the conference. The two brawlers were still fast asleep. All of England was still asleep. Only the mad, the missionaries and the milkmen who deliver the milk to the front door were on the road at such a time.

"I introduced the workshop with the following word, "I want you to record everything you are now going to hear. These are the Lord's instructions to the mission. Thus sayeth the Lord." Attention was undivided for the next 45 minutes. We also read the scriptures that were whispered to me but were unknown to me up to that time. They underlined the message amazingly to the point.

"What subject had the Lord chosen? The workshop was on The Book of Mormon and how it was to be used in missionary work. Three days after the first zone conference, President Spencer W. Kimball, then the Church's prophet, died. Five days later Ezra Taft Benson was sustained as the new president of the Church. Interestingly, on the same day at a press conference, he said, 'The Church is under condemnation, because it does not use The Book of Mormon as designed by the Lord. We must flood the earth with The Book of Mormon.' I was in tears. The Lord conveyed to me the same message the week before. The content of the workshop was indeed the will and the voice of the Lord (see Doctrine and Covenants 68:4).

"On January 21st 1986, Elder Jörgen Manhammar, an outstanding Swedish Zone Leader, reported that after that zone conference he and his companion had begun to read more in The Book of Mormon while teaching. They had been teaching a certain father for a long time but he hadn't yet joined the Church. They started to read from The Book of Mormon in every teaching situation. On the Sunday before Christmas, just before leaving for a three-week holiday, the father accompanied his family to church and said to the missionaries, 'We are leaving for a vacation now, but as soon as we get back, I will immediately set a date for my baptism.' This man was baptised on January 14th, 1986. His wife and their children were on cloud nine."

The Lord blesses the missionaries when they give heed to His word and act upon it, and on this occasion, He blessed a humble missionary who was seeking His will.

# CHAPTER 9

# FOLLOW THE LORD'S AGENDA

*"And the reason why he ceaseth to do miracles among the children of men is because that they dwindle in unbelief, and depart from the right way, and know not the God in whom they should trust." (Moroni 9:20).*

Sometimes as missionaries we spend a lot of time trying to find new ways and ideas to share the gospel more successfully, and bring as many of Heavenly Father's children as possible into His Kingdom. Certainly, preparation and planning are necessary, but they won't probably work, or won't be so effective if we don't get the Lord involved.

In other words, if we rely mostly on our judgment and our agenda, we won't see as much success as if we rely on Him and sought to connect to His agenda. Sometimes we forget that He is in charge and that He knows perfectly what's going on in His children's lives. He works with them continually to help them to be ready to accept the gospel when the opportunity comes.

Let me share an experience. In one of the cities where I served, my companion and I decided that we would do our best to team up with the Lord and seek His guidance as we set goals for our first month together.

Every morning we made a deal with the Lord. Our part of the deal was to commit to accomplishing certain goals during the day and His part of the deal was to inspire us to know exactly where to go to be able to accomplish these goals and find those people who were ready at the very moment.

For example, we set goals on the number of copies of The Book Mormon we wanted to place, the number of people we wanted to add to our teaching pool or speak with. We then prayed together each morning asking Heavenly Father to direct us to a certain area and as we looked at the map, we waited for the Lord to tell us where to go.

I can testify that every single day during that month together we accomplished our goals, and at the same time we were able to find many who were ready and were baptised.

One evening, we were still short of one first discussion to meet our daily goal, so we felt inspired to knock on a few more doors in a residential neighbourhood. We were exercising our faith that someone would invite us in. Believe it or not someone did invite us in, and we taught the first discussion.

As we witnessed the hand of the Lord manifesting regularly in our daily work, our confidence in Him and ourselves grew stronger to the point that we felt that we were indeed working shoulder to shoulder with the Almighty God, even us simple and humble missionaries.

So, remember, He is in charge. Work with Him! Work for Him! Follow His agenda and you will see great miracles in your life and the lives of those whom you are called to serve.

Wilford Woodruff, one of the most successful missionaries who laboured in England, once declared, "The whole history of this Herefordshire mission shows the importance of listening to the still small voice of the spirit of God, and the revelations of the Holy Ghost. The people were praying for light and truth, and the Lord sent me to them" (In Cowley, *Wilford Woodruff*, p. 118). He certainly followed the Lord's agenda and by doing this he was able to be guided to hundreds of people who were ready to accept the gospel.

Moroni taught the following, "And if there were miracles wrought then, why has God ceased to be a God of miracles and yet be an unchangeable Being? And behold, I say unto you he changeth not; if so he would cease to be God; and he ceaseth not to be God, and is a God of miracles.

"And the reason why he ceaseth to do miracles among the children of men is because that they dwindle in unbelief, and depart from the right way, and know not the God in whom they should trust.

"Behold, I say unto you that whoso believeth in Christ, doubting nothing, whatsoever he shall ask the Father in the name of Christ it shall be granted him; and this promise is unto all, even unto the ends of the earth" (Moroni 9:19-21).

So, is He still a God of miracles today just like He was at the time of Moroni and Wilford Woodruff? I testify that He will be if you have faith in Him and follow His inspired agenda.

# CHAPTER 10

# BECOME AN INSTRUMENT
# IN THE LORD'S HANDS

*"And he said unto them, 'This kind can come forth by nothing, but by prayer and fasting" (Mark 9:29).*

One of my favourite passages of scripture is the healing of the Saviour of the boy described by his father as having a dumb spirit whom the disciples hadn't been able to cure. They certainly exercised their faith and used the priesthood, but they weren't able to make him whole.

The Saviour rebuked the devil and it departed out of boy immediately. I am sure that the disciples were disappointed as they hadn't been able to heal the boy, so they asked the Master to explain why. The answer from the Lord was clear and straight to the point, "This kind can come forth by nothing, but by prayer and fasting" (Mark 9:29).

One of the things I have learned on my mission is that, at times, it takes an extra effort to see the arm of the Lord manifested, just like the disciples found on this occasion.

Let me share a personal experience with fasting and prayer that I had as a missionary hoping you see how powerful and inspirational fasting with a purpose can be.

At one time, we had an investigator who was progressing well towards baptism. She accepted all the principles we taught and she was already keeping the commandments, including tithing. However, when we challenged her to be baptised, she backed off and refused. We were shocked as she was just a golden friend, but there was something along the way that we couldn't quite figure out.

During our subsequent visit with the local bishop we agreed to fast and pray together so that she could overcome whatever problem, fear or doubt she had. We started fasting on Saturday evening, aiming to fast for twenty-four hours and to meet her at church as usual.

Although I wasn't feeling well, I decided to fast anyway as it was so important to help and support her at such a crucial time. I know it was a bit silly to fast in my condition, but I was anxious that she should receive the inspiration she needed to overcome whatever was preventing her from being baptised.

When we arrived at church she was there, and as we attended sacrament meeting all seemed to be proceeding well. However, during the second hour whilst we were all gathered for the Gospel Principle class, she suddenly got up and began to run away.

Of course, we were taken by surprise and didn't know what to do. We even thought of chasing her to find out what was happening, but then we decided we should give her some time and space, and call by later.

As we began to walk back home, my physical condition began to worsen. I felt tired and I could feel my body temperature going up. We made our way home and to our great disappointment we found a bag on our doorstep with all the books and pamphlets we had given this investigator with a note saying, "Thank you Elders for what you have done but please don't come to see me anymore." We just couldn't believe what we were reading.

"How is it possible?" we asked ourselves.

"I can't believe it," exclaimed my companion.

With sad hearts we made our way in, and we sat in the living room trying to make sense of what was happening.

50

Then my companion very conscious of hungry he was said, "Elder it's clear that it's over now. Let's finish our fast. You aren't feeling well and there is no reason to continue."

After thinking for a moment, I said, "Elder, I understand how you feel, I'm sad, too. However, our fasting isn't over yet. There are still a couple of hours. Let's exercise faith till the end".

At this point I was so weak that I decided to lie in bed for a while just to recuperate a bit of strength. I had scarcely done so when I immediately felt overcome and fell asleep. During my short sleep, I had a dream. In the dream I saw our investigator. She was crying and kept begging me to go back. I sat immediately in my bed, and exclaimed to my companion, "Elder, we need to go back".

He replied straightaway saying, "Elder, are you crazy? Don't you remember that she has left a note where she told us to leave her alone?".

I paused for a second and then I said, "Elder, I know where you are coming from, but the Lord has told me to go back and we will go back!". He continued to express his concerns as we got ready to go out accusing me of lack of respect, so on and so forth. However, nothing could have stopped me from going back.

It had been too clear for me. If I didn't follow up, I would regret it for the rest of my life. As we were making our way towards her home. I didn't know what to expect, but I was following a clear prompting from the Lord with full trust in Him.

When we arrived at her place, we rang the bell holding our breath, waiting for her to open the door. As she opened the door, we realised that she was in tears. Before we could utter any word, she said, "Elders, I thought I would never see you again. I kept praying all afternoon that somehow you would come back."

You can imagine how I felt at that moment. The Spirit overtook my whole being completely, so much so that I couldn't say anything for a little while. When I finally recovered from such an outpouring of the Spirit, I told her that we were happy, too, to have come back and that the Lord had answered her prayer by inspiring us to go back.

What a miracle! That evening she opened up and shared with us what was holding her back. A few weeks later she and her children were all baptised.

When I reflect on this experience, I can't help thinking what would have happened if we had stopped fasting at the first test of our faith. Would we ever have received revelation? Would we have received revelation to go back? Would we have seen her again? I testify that because we didn't give up when things seemed to go against us we were able to access the powers of heaven and witness a miracle in the life of this wonderful lady and her family.

I encourage you to seek extra help through fasting and prayer to access the powers of Heaven and use them to bless your life and the lives of those whom you will serve.

# CHAPTER 11

# THE POWER OF PRAYER

*"If any of you lack wisdom, let him ask of God, that giveth to all men liberally, and upbraideth not; and it shall be given him" (James 1:5).*

When the prophet Joseph Smith read the famous verses in the epistle of James, he realised that the only way to find the answers to his questions was to ask of God.

We are all familiar with his story and what happened because of his search for truth through prayer, so I would like to use his experience to illustrate this point.

First, he chose the time of the day (morning) when his mind was clear of any worldly thoughts and refreshed from a good night's sleep. Second, he selected a place where he could be alone and concentrate on his effort to ask of God. Third, he poured out the desires of his heart to God. What happened after this has changed the world forever.

I believe that too often, we don't follow these important steps when we approach God for guidance or inspiration and, by so doing, we limit the potential to receive the knowledge we are seeking.

If you want to receive the help you need in your search for people who are ready to accept the gospel you *must* get on your knees and seek for divine guidance and inspiration just like Joseph did.

As you recall, Alma and the sons of Mosiah sought to obtain the word with much praying and fasting so that their tongues could be loosed, and they could be endowed with the power to convince people of their message. What we learn from them is that this power is something to be sought. In other words, it doesn't come automatically with the calling package.

Alma the Younger and the sons of Mosiah knew too well that, unless they spent quite some time on their knees, they would never ever have a chance to bring the Lamanites, who were their worst enemies, to the knowledge of their Redeemer.

On my mission, prayer, sometimes combined with fasting, was fundamental in unlocking the doors that allowed my companions and me to find those who were seeking truth.

One of my companions, Elder Humphrey, (the same companion who wrote the letter mentioned at the beginning of this book), shared with me what he did later during his mission to seek to obtain the word and inspiration from the Lord. (You can read the story in his own words in the letter – appendix 1).

He told me about a room on the third floor of a flat he lived in with some other missionaries. His description made it clear that it was an unpleasant environment, damp, musty and mouldy. A place to avoid if possible.

However, that room became a special place for him as he used to spend quite a bit of time there, pouring out the desires of his heart to God. Entering this room was for him, and for the other missionaries who lived in the flat, like entering the presence of God. It was here that they found close communion with Him and received answers to their prayers.

One day, he was having a hard time because the work was not going well in the area, and he very much wanted to be transferred elsewhere. So, with this desire in his heart, he went to the room to plead with God. He spent almost an hour on his knees, supplicating the Lord and seeking guidance to help him through this difficult time.

What occurred during this time changed his mission drastically and made a huge difference, from that time forward, to his approach to missionary work. He finally received an answer to his prayers, which gave him the comfort and knowledge he needed, as well as helping him to recapture the vision of why he was serving there, and what the Lord expected of him. It was a sacred experience that dramatically changed his approach to missionary work and affected him for the rest of his mission.

So, get on your knees as much as you can, and don't be afraid to bruise them! This is where you will find the inspiration and guidance you will need to overcome your difficult times. It is also where you will be able to receive the revelation you need in your quest to find those who will hear your message.

# CHAPTER 12

# FEAR NO MAN

*"...perfect love casteth out fear..." (1 John 4:18).*

This is a scripture that often comes to my mind.

Let me share an example that can illustrate this principle. If a member of your family was in danger, wouldn't you intervene straightaway at whatever cost? What would move you to immediate action even despite the danger? The answer is very simple. Love is the motivating force that would give you the strength and the courage to face any challenge, even at the cost of your life, to protect your loved ones.

If you translate this into missionary work, isn't love perhaps the moving force that would spark in you the desire to share the gospel with your family and friends?

The sons of Mosiah certainly understood this principle, and felt this love when they decided to leave everything behind to serve a mission of fourteen years amongst the Lamanites who were their bitter enemies instead.

We read that, "Now they were desirous that salvation should be declared unto every creature, for they could not bear that any human soul should perish; yea, even the very thoughts that any soul should endure endless torment did cause them to quake and tremble" (Mosiah 28:3).

Why did they feel this way? Why did the very thought that even one of the Lamanites could be lost make them tremble? I am convinced that it was because of their love for these people which was stronger than any fear or worry.

Perfect love did indeed cast out fear.

"I fear no man" was one of my mottos throughout my mission. No one and nothing could stop me from achieving my purpose of reaching out to everyone who would come across my path, or whom I would feel inspired to stop.

I often felt the love that Heavenly Father has for his children, and I firmly believe this was what gave me the conviction that I had nothing to fear. It was what gave me the boldness to declare to anyone, even kings or rulers if I had had the chance, the good news of the restored gospel of Jesus Christ.

For me, it was a matter of spiritual life or death, and this feeling of urgency grew stronger and deeper every day until the end of my mission. I often thought about how it was possible for me, a humble missionary to experience such great love. I believe that it was because I had a desire to feel it and to put it into action during my time as a missionary.

Moroni taught, "Wherefore, my beloved brethren, pray unto the Father with all the energy of heart, that ye may be filled with this love, which he hath bestowed upon all who are true followers of his Son, Jesus Christ..." (Moroni 7:48).

I sought this gift throughout my mission, and I was blessed to feel it, even if to a small degree. Still it was enough to spur me on and keep the flame of love burning as well as a lively desire to share the gospel.

I remember one evening as I was returning home with my companion, I was confronted by a drunk man, who started to yell in my face. He was literally 2 centimetres away from my nose. He was mad at me for no reason and wouldn't let me pass.

As my companion and I remained calm, he continued to insult us and to keep us from walking away. Then he asked us what we were doing in the UK. I realised that for some reason he was mad at us because he thought we were both American.

At this point I strongly felt the Spirit of the Lord and His love for this man. So, I said, "We are to teach the Gospel of Jesus Christ to the wonderful people of England like you!" I could tell straight away that he was impressed, even in his drunken state and that he had been touched by my calm answer and by the sincere love I was showing.

He immediately backed off and let us go. I met this man other times along our way back to our flat. We became pretty good friends, and even though I wasn't able to teach him the gospel of Jesus Christ, I am sure that a seed was planted in his heart to blossom in its due time.

"Paul wrote to Timothy: 'God hath not given us the spirit of fear; but of power, and of love, and of a sound mind. Be not thou therefore ashamed of the testimony of our Lord'" (2 Timothy 1:7-8). 'President Hinckley declared', "...I wish that every member of this church would put those words where he might see them every morning as he/she begins his/her day. They would give us the courage to speak up. They would give us the faith to try. They would strengthen our conviction of the Lord Jesus Christ..." (Church of Jesus Christ of Latter-day Saints, *Teaching of Presidents of the Church: Gordon B. Hinckley*, p.338).

I urge you to seek this gift and use it to fuel your desire to serve and to keep the flame of your testimony burning, so that it can be a mighty instrument in the Lord's hands.

# CHAPTER 13

# BE BOLD

*"Use boldness, but not overbearance" (Alma 38:12).*

I always believed that overbearance is boldness without love. Alma counselled his son Shiblon, as he encouraged him to continue to teach, to, "Use boldness and not overbearance...".

In other words, we need to find a balance between these two extremes of communication, with other people. I am convinced that Shiblon was facing similar situations to those that you are facing now, or you may be facing in the mission field. Perhaps he was too forceful, too overwhelming in his approach. How can you be bold enough and avoid failing to speak the truth because you fear the reactions of other people? And how can you avoid coming across as too pushy or as showing lack of respect?

As I mentioned in the previous chapter, first, you need to cultivate a desire to develop the gift of charity and apply it in your daily life both with your companions and with the people out there. You will gradually see that, as this Christlike love grows in you, you will begin to look at people literally as your brothers and sisters.

Because of this, you will develop a genuine, kind and loving approach toward them, including the courage to stand as a witness at all times and in all places. You will feel a natural disposition to open your mouth, and to convey this same love to those with whom you will be sharing the gospel. You will learn to put your trust in the Lord and to be brave as His ambassador.

When I was a missionary, I sometimes struggled to find a balance between boldness and overbearance. Frankly, I leaned more toward boldness, which was what gave me the strength and the confidence that there was nothing to fear, and that I could share my message no matter who was in front of me.

I believe I spoke with a very wide range of people whose paths I crossed. These people included priests, ministers of religion, religious fanatics, policemen, traffic wardens, bus drivers, lollipop wardens, people running, people on bikes, people on the bus, people waiting for the bus, people working in stores, people in stores, people barbequing, people playing sports, doctors, nurses in hospitals, dentists, street cleaners, teachers, students, lawyers, the homeless, and so on.

Believe me, my friend, there is no need to fear. Don't forget that you are on the Lord's side, that you have been called and set apart to teach and baptise Heavenly Father's children. You are carrying in your hands the most important message that the world has ever heard, together with eternal blessings for individuals and families. God is at the helm! You don't need to fear. Be courageous, be bold, be loving and you will see great wonders wrought by the Lord through you.

Maybe you are shy or not a people person. Perhaps you think that you're different from me, that I was a bold person to start with. I can tell you, that wasn't the case.

As I was growing up, I loved to play with other children, but I was a bit insecure. I loved playing football and was good at it. However, there were times when I didn't show up for matches because I was scared that I wouldn't play a good game. So, I did have my insecurities, I still do. Who doesn't? When I was on my mission, it was different. I felt as though with God's help I could do anything.

This makes me think of prophets like Moses. He had a speech impediment and wasn't a dynamic speaker. I am sure he might have felt inadequate because of some physical limitations. Did these limitations stop him to do great things with God's help? No!

So, if you think you are shy, insecure or inadequate, remember you are not alone in this work! You are doing His work and if you search for His guidance, He will help you all the way.

When the sons of Mosiah began their journey in the wilderness, they sought help from Heavenly Father so that they could have a portion of His Spirit, and become instruments in His hands to bring the Lamanites to repentance. We read that "...the Lord did visit with His Spirit and...they were comforted and... [their hearts] took courage to go forth and declare unto them the word of God.

After the angel rebuked Laman and Lemuel for smiting their younger brothers, he told them to go up to Jerusalem again and Laban would be delivered into their hands. What did they do? They began to murmur again.

They said, "...How is it possible that the Lord will deliver Laban into our hands? Behold, he is a mighty man, and he can command fifty, yea, even he can slay fifty; then why not us?" (1Nephi 3:31).

Now, we often judge these two men, but since Laban had already rejected the brothers twice, and had tried to take both their property and their lives, their concern about returning is understandable, especially considering Laban's power. But Nephi, a man of great faith, taught them that God was mightier than Laban and even all of his tens of thousands. So, they didn't give up.

Now, perhaps you may feel like Laman and Lemuel as you approach people to share the gospel. Perhaps this fear of rejection immobilises you, so that you freeze up and you are not able to express your full potential as a missionary. You might think the people you are teaching aren't interested in religion. You may think they don't like Mormons or you might think that rich people aren't receptive to the gospel.

Maybe you could list all your limiting beliefs so that you can challenge them. Believing that you can't be successful limits you, just as it did Laman and Lemuel.

But Nephi trusted in the Lord so he went back to Jerusalem not knowing beforehand what he should do. "And I was led by the Spirit, not knowing beforehand the things which I should do" (1 Nephi 4:6). The rest is history. He made it. Was he scared? Yes. Was he worried? Yes, but he trusted in the power of God who made him mightier than all.

If you will do the same, Heavenly Father will make you a powerful instrument in His hands to do a wonderful work during your time as a fulltime missionary and for the rest of your life. Just believe it!

# CHAPTER 14

# LET THE SPIRIT GUIDE YOU

*"For the Holy Ghost shall teach you in the same hour what ye ought to say" (Luke 12:12.)*

One of the main temporal challenges during my mission was to keep my bike in good shape. I ended up at the bike shop quite often to fix it. On one of these occasions, when my companion and I were both getting our bikes fixed, I suddenly felt a strong impression to leave the shop.

Whilst I was inside the shop, I suddenly felt a clear and strong impression to go out of the shop. Now, you know that missionaries aren't allowed to leave their companions and must at least keep eye contact when they are working in the street.

My immediate reaction was to be obedient and stay with my companion inside the shop, so I tried to ignore the impression. However, it became so overwhelming that I decided to surrender and went into the street.

When I went out, I kept looking at my companion who wasn't far inside the shop and, at the same time, I started to look around searching for something that would help me figure out the reason for such a strong impression. As I checked with my companion to ensure that everything was all right, he gave me the thumbs up reassuring me that he was fine.

Then I looked to my right, and as I did so I noticed a woman who was walking in the opposite direction. She was wearing headphones, so I assumed that she was listening to some music. Here I was in the middle of the street looking at this woman and keeping an eye on my companion who was still in the shop. Was she the reason I had been impressed to leave the shop?

As I stood there trying to figure what on earth was going on, I was struck by a very strong impression that she was indeed the reason. But what could I do? My companion was still in the shop and she had reached the end of the road, so she was about to turn right and disappear.

Shouting wouldn't have helped as she was wearing headphones, so I prayed that she would stop and turn. At this point she turned, so I started to wave vigorously to attract her attention.

By now, my companion had left the shop, so we started to walk together towards her. To our surprise, she started to walk toward us, too, so we met halfway. When we finally got close enough, I exclaimed, "I am so glad you turned around. You know I kept looking toward you and I prayed that you would turn so that we could talk to you."

She replied with a little bit of emotion in her voice, "Elders, as I was walking and listening to music I kept feeling that I had to turn back but I was running late to an appointment, so I ignored the feeling until it became too strong.

As she shared her side of the story, I couldn't help shedding a few tears as I realised what the Spirit had done to allow us to connect in such a miraculous way. This wonderful lady was ready to accept the gospel. She had been prepared by the Lord to be found at the right moment and in the right place. She took the lessons, was baptised and brought four friends into the Church in the following couple of weeks.

This pattern of receiving clear promptings and acting upon them accompanied me throughout my mission. I do know that as I learned to recognize how the Spirit worked through me, it became quite simple to follow His promptings.

Believe me, if it weren't for the Spirit, I would not have found the people that I did. The credit goes entirely to Him. What I am saying is that doing your best to be tuned in to the Spirit will enable you to be guided to as many people as possible.

Heavenly Father knows His children and works with them independently to prepare them for the gospel. If you seek the Spirit, and rely on His guidance, you can be at the right place and at the right time when they are ready. It's like connecting to a radio station. Unless you seek to find the right signal by turning the dial, you won't find the right radio station you are looking for and enjoy beautiful music.

So, what can you do to receive such special help? Of course, prayer and scripture study are critical to gain knowledge and align with the Spirit of the Lord. Certainly, obedience to the commandments and the mission rules is also key to qualifying for this special guiding hand.

However, this is not enough. You need to believe absolutely that the power of the Spirit is real and can guide you to those who are ready to accept the gospel. Then the Lord can use you as His instrument, and you can witness the greatest number of wonderful experiences possible in your own life, and in the lives of those you serve.

# CHAPTER 15

# BE CREATIVE

*"A man's gift maketh room for him, and bringeth him before great men" (Proverbs 18:16).*

During my mission, I found that using creativity to the full helped me improve my approach, and opened many doors.

Now, don't get me wrong, you don't have to show up in some superhero outfit or wearing a blond wig. I'm not suggesting resorting to gimmicks, but I do believe you need to think outside the box and try to create an immediate connection with the people at the door or in the street. Let me share a few examples.

Once when we were knocking on doors, I wanted to find something that would immediately create a connection with the person who opened the door. So, when this guy came to the door, I looked for a hint that I could use in my approach. I looked into the house when the next door was opened, and noticed a painting on the wall. 'What a beautiful painting that is, sir,' I said. 'I have a similar one at home. Who is the artist?' The man told me, and remarked on the coincidence. As our conversation continued, he led me into the house. So, here we were inside without even making any mention of the reason why we had knocked on his door. The next step came very easily. "Do you mind if we share a short message about Jesus Christ?" Having created a connection with him, he was happy to allow us to stay and deliver our message.

On another occasion we decided to play a game. We called it "A Book of Mormon from Heaven." It went like this. I stood in front of the door, and when it was opened, I would look up and say, "A Book of Mormon from heaven! My companion would throw the book over into my hands, to the astonishment of the person at the door. This usually resulted in a good laugh, and an invitation to share our message.

One last example. On this occasion we were tracting under the snow after having spent most of our morning street contacting. As tracting isn't the most amusing thing to do, I decided to play a game with my companion.

The game consisted in giving your companion one or more than one word to use in the door approach. When my turn arrived, my companion gave me the words Joseph Smith to use.

Now, if you think about it for a minute, Joseph Smith isn't someone you would mention in a door approach, but I had no alternative and I had to come up with something creative. I introduced myself and my companion to the man at the door and said, "Good afternoon Sir, we are missionaries of the Church of Jesus Christ of Latter-day Saints, my name is Joseph Smith, and this is my companion Brigham Young".

You should have seen my companion's face. He didn't say anything, but his eyes were speaking for him and the message was, "Are you crazy?" Well, after a few seconds of uncertainty this man said, "Come in guys, it's cold outside". As we got in my companion kept nudging me and looking at me still questioning my door approach.

However, as we sat down with this man and his family, we soon realised that their last name was Smith. Now, as they never commented or remembered the names

I used to introduce ourselves, we thought it was a good idea to avoid bringing it up.

Suffice it to say that this was a golden family. A few weeks later they all entered the waters of baptism. I know these episodes may seem a little crazy, especially the last one, but my point is that you need to be creative if you are to make a connection with people so that you are able to deliver your message.

So, how can you be more creative ? What are some of the talents that you have been blessed with? For example, if you are an artist, how can you use your gift to improve your finding and teaching skills? If you are a sportsman, how can you use your physical abilities to enhance your missionary strategies?

The Saviour Himself was very creative when he taught during His ministry. There are many examples in the scriptures showing how He used the natural elements around Him to teach the people. He didn't have a strict structure that He followed. He was flexible in the way He conveyed His message using metaphors and parables to help Him better illustrate His points and touch people's minds and hearts.

He was a magnet to people, because He made connection by using elements that they were familiar with. He spoke about things that resonated with them.

So, feel free to be yourself, to be authentic, the real you. It is always the best way to connect with people and they will in turn listen to what you have to say.

# CHAPTER 16

# WORK WITH LOCAL LEADERS AND MEMBERS

*"Now it is the time for members and missionaries to come together, to work together, to labor in the Lord's vineyard to bring souls unto Him" (President Thomas S. Monson, Welcome to Conference, Oct 2013).*

I think that it's very clear from President Monson's quote, that he felt members and missionaries need to work together to see the work of salvation growing exponentially. The question is why is it not happening yet?

Once while I was training a group of missionaries, I asked them what their assumptions were regarding working with members. What they affirmed was quite surprising. The majority of them weren't doing any work with members, because they didn't think that they were converted and therefore, it would have been a waste of time.

I know from personal experience that this attitude would limit your sphere of action and success as a missionary. It would limit you because you would miss out on the great power there is when leaders, members and missionaries work together.

As I am writing this book, we are in lockdown because of COVID -19. Missionaries around the world have been asked to stay at home, and they are encouraged to use social media to find new people and thus increase their teaching pool. I notice that a lot of the missionaries are working with members globally to be able to have teaching opportunities and get referrals from them. So, now, that there aren't other finding tools available like street-contacting or tracting, missionaries are forced to work with the members. This would probably be their last option in normal times, at least in Europe.

I wonder if this is the reason why the Church isn't growing as it could. Is it because we, the members and the missionaries aren't working together as we should?

Think, for a moment, if the only finding resource were working with the members, what would be your approach? What would you do differently? It is certainly obvious that we aren't united in a coordinated effort.

What is the reason? It is because both missionaries and members are held back by negative assumptions. Perhaps, members, would even want to share the gospel but may not know how to do it. Maybe they think that the people they know aren't interested in the gospel or that they will never change. They may even fear to losing friends if they tell them about the Church, or to being judged or rejected because of their beliefs.

In conclusion, missionaries don't have confidence in the members and the members don't have confidence in themselves or in the missionaries. This negative approach from both sides is what is keeping us all from hastening the work at the pace the Lord expects.

Here's is what you need to do, in my opinion, if you want to work with members and leaders successfully and see great results during your mission.

First, you must work with your own recognised negative assumptions about members doing missionary work. You need to clear your mind from any biased thinking. You must begin working with members with faith, patience and an open mind.

I know that you would like to see results straight away. Sometimes working with the members doesn't produce much success in the short or medium term. However, if you are consistent in your attempt to work with them, results in the long term will be massively bigger and will change the destiny of the Church forever.

Second, you must build relationships of trust. Trust stands at the base of any relationship, including marriage, and those within the work and sports fields. If you manage to build a solid rapport with the members, then you have ninety percent of the job done. The other ten percent will be a walk in the park.

Of course, you need to be authentic and sincere. Otherwise you will obtain the opposite result. Once you have built this trust with the members then you will be in the position to overcome their assumptions by teaching them and showing them the way with patience and love.

Third and last, teach and train them concerning how they can share the gospel with their friends. Teach them how they can be involved in missionary work in other ways. For example, by using their home to teach, and taking members with you when you teach in investigators' homes. Ask them to pray for your friends, feed you, post on social media and as many other means that you can think of.

Although it's mentioned in the letter at the end of the book that I didn't work with members at the time I served with Elder Humphrey, I learned later on my mission to work with local leaders and members, and we witnessed miracles as we joined forces and worked together.

For part of my mission, I served in a little branch in the north of England. The unit was rather small and church meetings were held in a library, but the branch leaders were very committed and excited about missionary work.

I remember that the Elders' Quorum Presidency arranged missionary splits with us every single Wednesday, so, each week there were quite a few companionships who were going out to home teach, teaching our investigators or making visits to less active members.

I regularly went out with the Elders' Quorum President, a very good man who was truly engaged in the work. It was obvious from both his words and his actions that he loved the people he served deeply. I learned a lot from him, and it would be no exaggeration to say that he changed completely the way I look at people, as well as my appreciation for the kind of support and help we should provide to our church family.

Allow me to share an experience we had together when
we began visiting a woman, her husband and their daughter. The woman and her daughter were, at the time, less active members of the Church, but the man wasn't a member. He was an atheist so at the beginning we struggled to make any progress. We kept visiting them every week trying to build friendship and mutual trust.

Then something happened suddenly that completely changed the situation. The woman's mother, who was active in the Church, suddenly passed away. This was certainly a challenging time for the family but it also turned out to be a moment of change, as they began to wonder again about the purpose of life and especially life after death.

The man was particularly touched by the whole situation and began to gradually open his heart and ask questions as we continued to visit them each week.

Finally, they agreed to take the discussions, and as the Elders' Quorum President and I taught them, they gradually gained a desire to come to church. Finally, when the woman and her daughter returned to full activity again, the man decided to be baptised. What a miracle! I was particularly blessed to be present at his baptism even though I had been transferred to another area right before it.

Now, how did this whole thing come to pass? Certainly, the full credit goes to the Lord. He is the author of all conversions. He is the one who has the power to touch and to change hearts. However, we did our part together as a missionary and a leader with a common desire to love and bless the lives of Heavenly Father's children.

I hope that you will work closely with the members and with the leaders in the areas where you serve. This is the way to go forward if you want to contribute to hastening the work of salvation. I know that it works because I have witnessed it during my mission. You can do the same and encourage other missionaries to do likewise.

# CHAPTER 17

# WORK SMART

*"And it came to pass that I did make tools of the ore which I did molten out of the rock" (1 Nephi 17:16).*

When Lehi's family arrived at the ocean, the Lord asked Nephi to build a ship. Now, we don't know if Nephi or anyone else of his company were shipbuilders. This was a daunting task the Lord required of him. The family must have been even more anxious when they knew they would have to sail across an unknown ocean to an unfamiliar land.

How would you have felt if you were Nephi? Would you have looked for a way to build the ship or would you have dropped the ball and waited for something to happen miraculously?

Even though you will likely never be asked to build a ship, you may have to face similar challenges. There may be certain situations which could be as difficult and as daunting as the one Nephi experienced.

Certainly, Nephi relied a lot on the Lord's guidance and inspiration, but he also thought out of the box as he strove to find the necessary material and tools to build the ship. In other words, he worked smart, and, to accomplish his task, he went beyond his normal capacity and skillset.

During my mission I had my share of challenges and obstacles to overcome. I know that only by studying things out and taking them to the Lord was I able to find the needed solutions.

To illustrate my point, I will share the challenge that was presented to us in one of the areas where I served.

Because the church building was situated quite far from the main town, it was difficult to get there on Sundays when public transport was sporadic. This was a problem when we had investigators to take to meetings, and some of the members were facing the same issue.

All the odds were against us. However, we didn't give up. After much thinking and brainstorming we finally found what we were looking for. How on earth had we not thought about it before? We could hire a bus! It all made so much sense.

The bus could pick up everyone needing a lift to church on Sundays, including us and our investigators, and take everyone home afterwards.

We needed the ward leaders to approve our idea, which they did straightaway, so our problem, which had seemed insurmountable, was solved. What a blessing for everyone!'

Do you see what I mean? We could have given up at the first obstacle, but we continued to look for a solution, and it came. Therefore, whenever you find yourself confronted by a challenge or something difficult, don't give up but do your part until you find a way to accomplish what you want to achieve.

I am sure that with the Lord's help you will be able to overcome any obstacle in front of you, and accomplish your tasks no matter what. Like Nephi, if you are not afraid to build your boat and put your trust in the Lord, you will accomplish things that you would never have expected to do.

# CHAPTER 18

# A PRIESTHOOD BLESSING

*"...I will go before your face. I will be on your right hand and on your left, and my Spirit shall be in your hearts, and mine angels round about you, to bear you up"*
*(D&C 84:88).*

By the time I was a few months into my mission, President Kimball died, and President Benson was sustained as the new president of the Church of Jesus Christ of Latter-day Saints. His emphasis on the importance of The Book of Mormon became truly relevant to us as missionaries, and his invitation to flood the earth with copies of the book became our *theme.*

We decided that we would take his invitation to the letter, and place as many copies as possible. We would carry tens of copies of the book in our backpacks and refill later in the day if we ran out.

We were really on fire. Any occasion was a good one to give away a copy of the book. We were certain that if our investigators read The Book of Mormon, the odds that they would have joined the Church were considerably higher. So, we placed copies on buses and at bus stops, riding our bikes, at supermarkets, walking in the street and, of course, knocking on doors. We made a commitment that our area would be literally inundated with copies of the book and so we proceeded.

The promise from President Benson was clear. If our investigators read the book, the number of converts would grow exponentially. In his words, "The Book of Mormon is the instrument that God designed to sweep the earth and gather out His elect" (*Ezra Taft Benson, Welcome to Conference, Oct 1988*). We personalised the copies with our testimonies, and with the testimonies of the members. We also selected passages for our investigators to read, such as the Saviour's visit to the Nephites.

Unfortunately, my mission ended before I could witness this promise unfolding, but I know that the many were converted thanks to the power of The Book of Mormon.

A similar promise was given to other missionaries by President Boyd K. Packer years before, as told by Elder Christensen. Here's what he recorded on his mission journal.

"My new companion was Elder Gary Hutchinson from Heber City, Utah. He stood six foot six inches tall and weighed 295 pounds. You should have seen the looks on people's faces as we met them at the doors. We lived in the upstairs apartment #2 at 10 Nelson Street, Montpelier, Vermont. It was a little disappointing when I first arrived in Montpelier because there just didn't seem to be many houses to door contact. It was a much smaller town than Burlington had been.

"To make matters more complicated, I was now District Leader and I was responsible for two elders in Barre, Vermont and two near South Royalton in Norwich, Vermont, and a new companion from Utah. Elder Hutchinson and I got there the same day. We were told that the last baptism in the area had been more than a year ago when an eight year old boy had become of age and was baptized. My parents wrote the following: 'We kept hearing reports about Elders Rollins and Trent up in Burlington. One week they placed 45 copies of The Book of Mormon, the next week 66!' Everyone was amazed. They soon challenged us to a contest on the week of the

4th of July. We were really going to have to work hard, but I knew that we could beat them. One night I lay awake for several hours thinking about it. The more I thought about it, the more excited I got. If they could place 66, then we could place 100! It was possible and we were going to do it.

"We planned the whole week and arranged for our supplies. The two commitments we had for the week were both at the Joseph Smith Memorial. Wednesday we were having a District Leaders' Meeting and Thursday we were to be guides at the Joseph Smith Memorial Visitors' Center. Both would take most of the day, but we could and would work hard in the evenings. We had to do a certain amount every day to reach our goal of a hundred by the end of the week.

"Saturday night, the day before we were to begin the contest, Elder Hutchinson's feet began to bother him. It was too late to turn back now, so I took him to Barre and had him work that week with Elder Allred while Elder Brian Marsh, his new junior companion, worked with me.

"On the way home, I asked, 'How many copies of The Book of Mormon is it possible to place in a week?' He didn't want to disappoint me or show a lack of faith, so he said, 'Maybe 30.' I told him about the 66 that the Burlington Elders had placed, and he agreed that it was possible to place 66. I asked him if he thought we could place 100. He hesitated and said, 'Well, I suppose so. Sure, why not!' I said, 'That's what we're going to do this week.'

He was very excited when I told him about our preparations.

"By the time Sunday School started at 10:00 a.m. the next morning, we had placed 8 copies of The Book of Mormon. It was unbelievable! We were going to do it. At the end of the day, we had placed 33. What a day! I asked Elder Marsh what he knew. He was so excited and in wonderment said, 'I don't know very much, but I do know that we can place 33 copies of The Book of Mormon in one day!'

"We set our goal up to 34 for the next day. Monday morning, we started contacting at 8:00 a.m. and worked until 9:30 or 10:00 p.m. that night. We spent very little time eating dinners. Our diet for breakfast consisted of oatmeal and fried perch. Our lunch was sandwiches made out of a fish spread that we made by poaching the fish and mixing it with salad dressing. Our dinners also consisted of vegetables and perch cooked some other way. The Smiths had provided us with a big mess of fresh perch from Lake Champlain that helped us survive the week.

"We set our goals for placing a certain amount before lunch, so many in the afternoon and so many after supper at night. To meet those smaller goals, we discovered that we needed to place so many each hour. Our goals helped us tremendously. Monday, we placed our 34 and Tuesday 35. We had already reached and passed our original goal and the week wasn't even half over yet. We ordered another 100 copies and set a new goal at 200! We were really working as a team. We wasted no time and tried to refine our door approaches, to be more effective. Our appointment book was bulging with callbacks. We needed a lot of help the next week teaching all the discussions.

"Saturday was terrific! It was our last day and we had placed copies of The Book of Mormon in 15 houses in a row. The Lord was with us and we could feel his influence. We needed to place 27 total that day to reach our final goal of 200. By noon it was 19 for 23 homes. We had placed 15 for 15 before someone said no.

"We were contacting on the highway going up to

Stowe, Vermont. Our throats were a little raspy and we didn't want to be too mechanical in our approach, so we decided to try to teach a discussion at the next house to get a variety and little change of pace. We took our flannel board and flannel strips and taught first discussions in the next two homes and left copies of The Book of Mormon with them to read until we returned. It was so exciting, and the people were so nice that we felt like singing. We then went on down the road and met our goal in the later hours of the afternoon. We sent copies number 200 and 201 to our families as souvenirs.

"To my surprise Elders Thurgood and Webb in South Royalton area had placed (I think) 76 copies and Elders Allred and Hutchinson, in Barre, had placed 20! Elder Dennis Webb was also a new missionary since May. He had promise of being a great missionary. The total from our District was 297, more than the rest of the whole mission put together. The assistants asked if we had been dumping them in the river or giving them away. We had only given 7 away and several of those later paid for them. Some said our record could or would never be broken, but we knew it could.

"I was transferred to Augusta, Maine as a new Zone Leader. The missionaries had heard of what we had done and wanted to know the details. In our first Zone meeting I explained, but one doubtful Elder asked if the story was really true. I testified that it was and said, 'If we have enough faith, we could place 100 in one day!'

"With a grin on his face, he said, 'Show me!'

During our lunch break I took him to a large hotel, and we got a picture of us giving a copy to the manager and permission to place 120 copies in all the hotel rooms. When we got back to the meeting, the Elder told the others that if he had not seen it with his own eyes, he would not have believed it could be done.

"Well, President Packer's promise was fulfilled. He had promised us that if our Book of Mormon placement went up our convert baptisms would also go up. In the three months that we were in Montpelier, 17 people were baptized in our branch that had not had a single baptism in four years. The last recorded convert baptism had been the Branch President's son who was nine years of age and qualified to be counted as a convert baptism.

"The Lord had not forsaken us. The Smiths (Sister Virginia and daughters Christina and Rebecca and son Mark), Brother Clifton King, the Ayers (Patrick and Florence and children: Patricia, James, Dean, Daniel, Alberta and David) and the Edsons (James and Sue Ann), Sister Winnifred Corbett and Sister Christina Magoon all were baptized.

As you can see from these stories The Book of Mormon is the best tool that you can use to find those of Heavenly Father's children who are looking for the Gospel. It's the keystone of our religion and, as the prophet Joseph Smith put it, "...a man would get nearer to God by abiding by its precepts, than by any other book."

I encourage you to use it and as you challenge the people you will find to read it and ponder its content, they will, as Moroni promised, know the truth of it by the power of the Holy Ghost (see Moroni 10:4-5)..

# CHAPTER 19

# HOW DO YOU MEASURE SUCCESS?

*"...I do not glory of myself, but I glory in that which the
Lord hath commanded me; yea, and this is my glory, that
perhaps I may be an instrument in the hands of God to
bring some soul to repentance; and this is my joy"*
*(Alma 29:9)*

The tendency people have in the world, and especially
in business, is to measure success by actual performance.
For example, we measure success in the number of sales,
increased profit, or business growth. How do you measure
success in the Lord's work?

I can honestly say that, in the first part of my mission,
I struggled with the concept. For me, high numbers
equaled becoming a district or a zone leader and
eventually an assistant to the president.

Because I achieved outstanding numbers, but had not
yet been called as a district or zone leader, I questioned
the criteria the Lord was using when He made those
callings. Why had I not been called yet? What else did I
have to do?

This struggle with the Lord went on for a quite a
while. I was so caught up with this prideful thinking that I
would question the Lord all the time, so much so that it
became a stumbling block which kept me away from the
real spirit of service and the Spirit of the Lord.

One morning as I was taking a bath, I once again
raised my voice of complaint toward heaven and hassled

Heavenly Father with the same question. Why? I guess that He must have had enough of hearing me whining over and over again, because He finally decided that very morning to answer my question in a way that I shall never forget.

The Spirit spoke to me so clearly that it sounded like a man's voice, but more powerful. It pierced me to the core. He delivered the message that I needed to hear, "You have not chosen me, but I have chosen you. Stop asking this question. I am the one in charge."

I was petrified in the bathtub. He had just struck me with a powerful reproach. I remained speechless for quite a while pondering the content of His message and feeling terrible for my thoughts and behaviour. I surely needed to repent! The lesson was learned. From that moment forward I stopped thinking about these things and concentrated only on doing the work of the Lord, without aspiring to any particular position or leadership role. Funnily, opportunities to lead came once I stopped looking for them.

I have shared this personal experience because I want to warn you about aspiring to leadership positions during your mission. In the Lord's kingdom there is no hierarchy of importance depending on what calling you have. This includes anywhere in the mission field.

It doesn't make any difference where you serve but how you serve. The calling might be given to us to help us grow, because we need to have that experience or simply because the Lord needs us in that role.

In no way, does He discriminate between one or another because of the calling. Moreover, the simple fact that you have a leadership calling doesn't make you better than others. The same applies to you if you are not called. It doesn't make you worse than others.

I remember one time I asked a missionary what his role in the mission field was. He replied, "I am just a missionary!"

I told him, 'Just a missionary? Do you realise who you represent and the greatness of your calling as an ambassador of the Lord Jesus Christ?'

I hope that you value yourself as a missionary whatever your role may be. The opportunity to represent the Saviour is prestigious enough.

In other words, don't be bothered about callings or specific roles, just concentrate on your work. Do it with all your power, serve with all your heart. The Lord will accept your offer whatever your role will be. For Him it is enough that you have sacrificed part of your life to serve Him and His children, and that you have served him with all your heart, might, mind and strength.

There is nothing in this work to glory in yourself, but like Alma, you can glory in the knowledge that the Lord commanded and called you to be an instrument in His hands to bring some of His children back to repentance.

# CHAPTER 20

# YOU CAN MAKE A

# DIFFERENCE!

*"...If thou canst believe, all things are possible to him that believeth" (Mark 9:23).*

As a missionary of the Lord Jesus Christ, you have been called of God to labour to bring as many as possible of Heavenly Father's children to Christ. You will spend every waking hour for the duration of your mission finding, teaching and baptising those who are ready to accept the gospel.

Can you see the impact that you will have, or won't have, on some of His children? Indeed, you have been called to make a difference.

I hope that you will consider your mission as a unique opportunity to work shoulder to shoulder with Heavenly Father and Jesus Christ to bless the lives of the people you will search for and who will come across your path.

If you won't do it, who will? Will they have another opportunity if you let them pass by? Will they be able to enjoy the blessings of the gospel in their lives if you refrain from opening your mouth?

Think about all these things. How badly do you want to find the elect? What are you willing to put in the mix in terms of time, effort, and faith? Do you believe that your message can change lives? Do you have faith that the Lord can guide you to those who are ready to accept the gospel now? Do you want your mission to be full of great experiences and to see the hand of the Lord manifested in the lives of those whom you will be working with? Do you believe that miracles can still happen?

My dear friend, I hope that you will give much thought to your preparation and understanding of what a mission is all about, that you will trust the Lord, seek His guidance and work with Him. Love the people. Love your companions. Follow the Spirit and make your mission the best time of your life.

The magnitude of what you do will touch more lives than you can ever imagine. I would never have thought that my actions as a missionary would become examples to so many around the world. I still scarcely believe it. So, do your best to leave a legacy behind you that, perhaps, will continue to resonate in people's mind and hearts even beyond your time as a full-time missionary.

I hope that you believe you can make a difference in many people's lives, which will make a difference in yours, too. Be believing, dream big, work hard, work smart and you will witness great miracles throughout your service.

As you forget yourself in this service, you will let Heavenly Father refine you and make you a better disciple of Jesus Christ, and probably the biggest miracle you will witness will be within you!

Just one more thing. If you decide not to go on a mission, or are returning home before your time, I hope and pray that you won't carry shame for the rest of your life. Don't listen to what other people may say about it. Just keep in mind this simple truth, that God will not hold this against you, that He is more understanding than you think and that He loves you as much as if you had gone on your mission or finished the full service period.

# CHAPTER 21

# A LEARNING CURVE

*"You don't go through a mission; a mission goes through you" (Elder Don R. Clarke)*

When I think about my full-time mission, I think about a huge learning curve. I purposely want to use the adjective "huge" to describe the tremendous impact that my mission has had on my life and how it changed it forever. Every single day was a new opportunity for me to discover and learn about myself, God, the Saviour and the plan of salvation. It also began the process of transformation into a better disciple of Christ. This by the way, is still a work in progress.

A full-time mission is much more than just spending two years in a different country speaking a different language. Of course, it's nice to learn a new language, see different places and be exposed to a different culture, but that's not the reason why we serve missions.

I personally consider it like a super intense, unrepeatable masterclass training on almost anything that a person needs to learn and understand at spiritual, emotional, and psychological level.

A full-time mission multiplies exponentially anything learned, any experience lived, and any knowledge acquired. Nothing is like it. It's unique.

One of the most important things I have learned is that God is still a God of miracles, but to be able to access the powers of heaven, we need to exert great faith and trust in Him. He can do anything for us, whether it has to do with our missionary work, or our spiritual or temporal wellbeing, but we must be willing to do all we can. We must do all we can to connect with Him and tune in to the Spirit.

I have learned that He can't wait to show His power or to bless our lives and the lives of those we serve. We just need to believe and seek His guidance and inspiration.

I have also learned that He works with His children, our brothers and sisters, to prepare them to accept the gospel. He knows who they are and wants to show us where to find them. There is no doubt about that.

I have learned that salvation comes only through Christ, and that He is the one who heals, transforms, and changes people's lives if they let Him. I have learned that, as missionaries, we can be, and we have got to be, at the centre of this process, and we can facilitate this connection by serving as God's instruments so that He can do His job.

I have developed an understanding and a vision of the value that God places upon all of us, His children, and of the urgency of this work of salvation. The field is definitely white already to harvest *now*!

I have learned that God is a merciful God and that He loves and accepts our imperfections as they are. Sure, He wants us to improve, but He also takes us by His loving hand, and accompanies us during our mortal journey without stopping one single second to support us even when we fall, over and over again.

I have learned what God expects from me. I know I have failed Him at times and still do, but I also know that He can forgive and forget and allow me to start anew.

I have learned that my companions were at the top of the list of those whom I should love and serve, and that amongst the most important things I could accomplish as a missionary was to help them be better and closer to Christ after they left me.

I have learned that Jesus is my personal Saviour and Redeemer, that He bore my sins, imperfections, and sorrows so that I could return to live with Him again.

What would I be like if I hadn't served my mission? I can easily say that I wouldn't be the same person that I am. I mean, I am certainly far from perfection, my wife can confirm! However, my mission, as Elder Clarke said, went through me in such a powerful way as to completely change my nature and my relationship with God, and this has set the tone for the rest of my life.

If there is a secret to serving a mission I guess that this is it: let your mission, your relationship with God and the Saviour, as well as your experiences, create the changes to support you for the rest of your journey on earth. This will give you the strength, enthusiasm and commitment you need to continue along the covenant path back to Heavenly Father.

Going back to the statement at the beginning of this book, it is true that you need to prepare well for your mission so that it will be the experience it is supposed to be. In other words, it will be two years of intensive growth that will fill your spiritual reservoir and give you the boost to accomplish your mission on earth.

I will always be grateful to God for allowing me to serve shoulder to shoulder with Him, and to learn from Him as I humbly offered my time and energy to the gathering of the elect and to the building of His Kingdom, in the name of Jesus Christ, amen.

# APPENDIX

## THE RICCIARDI LETTER

By Danny Humphrey

Background.

This letter was originally written to Elder Clarke on June 17th, 1994, the son of a dear friend. I have updated this 16 year old letter with additional stories from my time as a missionary with Elder Ricciardi. The work any missionary does anywhere in the world is of critical importance to the development and conversion of the individual missionary. In other words, you.

Introduction.

I hope all is well and that your stay at the MTC has been the powerful spiritual experience that I remember. Upon returning from my mission I had the opportunity to teach at the MTC for almost 4 years while I was at BYU. My memories of the MTC are fond for both my mission experience and my post mission teaching experience. I wanted to write you and share some of the powerful lessons that I learned early in my mission that set the pace for the remainder of my time as a missionary.

When I arrived in England my very first companion (my trainer) was an Elder from La Spezia, Italy by the name of Elder Ricciardi. His full name was Fabrizio Giovanni Spartaco Ricciardi. Elder Ricciardi was an older missionary at 25 years old. He had joined the Church with his family 2 years earlier. He came from a very modest upbringing in what was mostly a farming community. I can honestly say that his personal influence and stubbornness in the early months of my mission shaped the way I approached missionary work for the remainder of my mission.

Train Ride to Loughborough.

We had been together about 2 hours when I caught a glimpse of what a spiritually powerful individual he is. We had boarded the train from Coventry station to Loughborough, which is a small town in the countryside of Leicestershire, England. In order to get to Loughborough, we had to change connections in the city of Birmingham.

The Birmingham train station is absolutely huge, and it was easy to see how one could quickly get lost if they were not familiar with the place. Ricciardi had checked a schedule he had in his pocket and we began to make our way to the platform. Once we reached our platform, I was overcome with jet lag and leaned against a wall to go to sleep. Our train was not due for an hour, so I thought a nap was in order. About fifteen minutes into the nap I awoke to see Ricciardi napping away against the back wall of the bench I was sitting on.

It was while I was staring at him that he suddenly bolted up from the bench and yelled at me to grab my luggage. He then took off down the ramp and turned the corner. He had startled me so much, that I quickly became angry and thought to myself, "When I catch up to him, he is going to get it!" I chased him up and down stairs and ramps before we reached a platform where a train was leaving right when we had gotten there. We literally jumped on the train as it was moving, just managing to get on safely before running out of the platform.

We found some seats, situated my luggage and finally sat down when I strongly inquired into what the heck he was doing jumping up from his nap and running me all over Birmingham train station. He told me that he was not napping, but in fact praying to the Lord for guidance. When we first entered the train station, we had stopped a passerby to inquire about platforms and were told to go to the platform we were at. While we were sitting at the platform Ricciardi felt uneasiness and decided to inquire of the Lord to confirm if we were at the right platform. The lateness of the hour and the fact that this was the final train for our area made accuracy of information imperative.

It was during his inquiry that a powerful impression came upon him, not only telling him that we had in fact been purposefully misled by our unknown passerby, but the Spirit, as clearly as Ricciardi was speaking to me, indicated where the correct platform was, and that the train was leaving right now! Hence the incredible chase. It was in the middle of his story that he stopped the train conductor to ask if we were in fact on the train to Loughborough. The conductor confirmed that it was and Ricciardi then fell asleep for the duration of the three hour train ride. I just stared at him for the remainder of the ride. First day in the Lord's vineyard and already a valuable lesson in spiritual discernment! From that day forward I saw the value of inquiring to the Lord *on all things*. Did I inquire of the Lord every day after witnessing that incident? No, I was human, but I certainly could tell the difference in my mission when I did.

Early to Rise.

I had been told at the MTC that as a new missionary normal wake up time is 6:30am, but that "greenie" missionaries (aka brand new missionaries) wake up at 6am. The earlier time is for getting the new missionary up to speed quicker through extra companion study. My very first morning, Ricciardi woke me up for companion study. I was so exhausted from jet lag, home sickness, running around the Birmingham train station at 30 miles per hour, I did not think to look at the time. In fact, the only method of telling time in our whole apartment was a wristwatch Elder Ricciardi wore. We studied, read scriptures, role played discussions then the same in personal study.

At the end of personal study, I was sure it had to be close to 9:30am departure time. I raced to get dressed, shaved, ironed shirt, tired but ready to go. Still in his pajamas, Elder Ricciardi looked at me and asked, "You look anxious to do the Lord's work… that is good."

I replied 'don't we have to go soon?'

He smiled. "Elder, we got up at 4:30am this morning; we have another 2 hours before we need to leave."

Now I was really angry. I opened the white missionary handbook (known as the white bible) and quoted to Elder Ricciardi, "Arise at 6:30am." He reminded me that for training purposes new missionaries were to arise earlier. "Tell me where it says 4:30am in the white handbook!" I inquired.

Elder Ricciardi calmly stood up and said "Elder, I am going to tell you a little secret. Most new missionaries are getting up at 4am. I chose 4:30am to give you a little extra rest. If you want to get up at 6:30am, I cannot control you. However, please know that we will be the only new missionary companionship in the whole mission not getting up early…I leave it up to you."

I certainly didn't want to be the only missionaries not getting up early… 4 weeks later we attended my first Zone Conference in the city of Nottingham. It was so much fun to see a few members of my MTC district. I went up to Elder Condor, my old MTC companion and said, "Isn't this getting up at 4:30am thing just a killer?" He looked at me like he had missed an easy to understand joke. So, he token laughed which I could tell meant he didn't get what I was talking about. I know a token laugh when I hear one. I said, "You know… getting up for companion study". He laughed again but this time it was the uncomfortable laugh, "Uhm, Elder Humphrey, what are you talking about? We get up at 6am." I was so mad. I immediately searched out 3 or 4 other new training companionships and confirmed what I had feared. Elder Ricciardi was killing me on purpose. I found Ricciardi in the chapel and gave him the business about being the only missionaries getting up at that crazy hour. He looked away from me, gave a long pause. Then he muttered, "Wow Elder, we are the only missionaries working hard in this whole mission…wonderful…that is good to know, nice work." I was speechless.

I Fear No Man.

Ricciardi had a saying that has stayed with me and will stay with me throughout my life. He would say to me, "I fear no man!" He spent his whole mission proving that slogan. Every day like clockwork 10 minutes before departure to proselyte, he would look in the bathroom mirror, point to it, and say "I fear no man". Then he would do it again with a different posture. I personally thought he was trying to make me laugh by doing it. You know… some inspirational thing for the new missionary. I soon learned he actually meant it. He was not kidding.

His door approaches were not only unique, but astounding. He would knock on a door, and when the door was answered he would introduce us as, "Missionaries from the Church of Jesus Christ of Latter-day Saints". As he would be giving his introduction, he would quickly look into the house to try and find something somewhere that would indicate some commonality that he could address in order to build relationships of trust.

One time, approximately the third or fourth day we had been together, a gentleman answered the door, looking really uptight about the fact that we were disturbing his quiet Saturday afternoon. During the opening dialogue Ricciardi glanced in the door and saw a beautiful painting on the wall. Suddenly, mid introduction, Ricciardi screamed out, "Oh what a beautiful painting!" pushed the door open (nearly sending the man through the wall) and walked right into the house. I stood on the doorstep in absolute horror, a witness to this unbelievable demonstration of bad manners. Ricciardi walked right into the living room, met the wife and kids, and admiring the television set they were transfixed by, commented "what a beautiful television, may we turn it off?" He hit the off switch. I was still on the porch, quite honestly waiting for the police to be called, or for him to get physically throw out of the house. To my shock I heard his thick Italian accent call down the hallway "Oh Elder Humphrey, will you join us?" I could not believe it. 45 minutes later we concluded the first discussion with a prayer. I confronted him later that night about the fiasco I had witnessed earlier in the day, he said, "Elder, I fear no man, and that includes you. I will do the Lord's work with or without you. I prefer with, but that is up to you."

Ricciardi expounded further, and I want you to remember this because it is absolutely true. Ricciardi told me the following, "Elder Humphrey, what is bold today, will not be bold tomorrow." He meant that what was uncomfortable for me to declare today, over time will become second nature, and not be seen as rude, but rather would be seen by others as conviction. He further stated that The Lord tells us in Alma 38:12 to be bold, but not overbearing. Ricciardi defined overbearance as boldness without love. When people know and feel your love, you can never be too bold, he would say. I would not have admitted it at the time because I was still too young and frankly immature to know, but it did not take me long to learn that his words that night were absolutely true.

The MTC, The Mission Field, and Follow Your Trainer. If you asked Ricciardi today about what it was like to have me as his companion, I am sure he would tell you that in the two months we spent together I was not humble, and did not buy into his way of doing missionary work. It is true, I fought him on stuff that I now look back with hindsight and realize was my pride and arrogance, and to a degree pure ignorance. Look, I loved the MTC, but to be frank, it is not the mission field. The MTC training is invaluable, but naturally it is limited, and when you finally do arrive in the field, you actually think you know quite a lot. After all you have spent three to eight weeks learning what you need to know about being a missionary. I capitalized the words to emphasize a bit of sarcasm. Truth is, you arrive knowing relatively little. Granted, you know more about gospel stuff than ever, but you still arrive fairly naïve to what the work involves. So, when your trainer tells you do this, don't say that, you pronounced, "Coriantumr" wrong it all gets under your skin.

The new missionary would like to feel acknowledged for something, for crying out loud you have spent a lot of time at the MTC preparing. Here is the deal that every missionary needs to know. Follow your trainer, because it is my contention that the most important calling in the mission field, even greater than Assistants to the President, Zone Leaders, District Leaders is hands down without question the Trainer. Why? Because they represent your introduction to the mission field, they set the pace of your missionary habits and disciplines. Post mission I worked at the MTC during a couple of training conferences for newly called Mission Presidents. In those training sessions mission presidents are instructed on how critical trainers are in the mission field. I trained once, Elder Degala was my greenie (meaning brand new missionary), and he would tell you today that we did not get along because I pulled a Ricciardi on him, and trained him the way Ricciardi trained me, which was demanding, full of boldness, and it drove him crazy because Degala had spent a lot of time in the MTC preparing.

Someone once commented, "Surely the legendary Elder Ricciardi was an Assistant to the President". No. In fact, he ended his mission a district leader (which he had been for a long time), never a zone leader, or AP. But here is what is mind boggling...he trained 4 times. Training more than once on your mission is very rare. In fact, I only know of one other missionary from our mission who trained three times. Training is the most difficult calling in the mission field. Elder Ricciardi trained 4 times! Why would the mission president not use Ricciardi in leadership positions such as AP or ZL? I'll tell you why, because every Mission President knows how vital a properly trained missionary is. Trainers make such a huge difference, taking what might have been a mediocre missionary and lighting a fire of confidence and spirituality. Our Mission President knew Elder Ricciardi's personal influence could be magnified by training 4 missionaries, who would train 4 more, who would train 4 more let alone the impact through future companionships of all those missionaries.

I met so many missionaries who were either trained by Ricciardi or had simply been companions. We all shared the same stories about his stubbornness, boldness, and spirituality. We differed on our feelings of getting along with him or not, but all unanimously agreed Ricciardi served a mission to the maximum extent a mission can be served, with all his might, mind, and strength. Ricciardi was too straight talking and bold (and I mean Italian Bold) to be an AP or ZL. He would have called down hell, fire and damnation on any missionaries not being obedient. That sort of condemnation should be left to the Mission President.

Nevertheless, never forget how important it is to obey your trainer and respect the calling of a trainer. I consider it the most important position of leadership in the mission field. By the way, if you by chance were paired with a lazy trainer who did not set the right pace for you, then please don't perpetuate that mistake when you become a trainer. A really bad trainer in the first months of a missionary's new life of dedicated service can snuff out an eager spirit. That is why it is without a doubt the most important calling in the mission field.

Continual Improvement

One night I learned the hard way about my pig-headedness regarding Ricciardi's methods. We had just finished teaching a young couple and on the bike ride home Ricciardi wanted to discuss how the lesson went and what we could do to improve. Ricciardi always wanted to review "how we did" right after a discussion and I often struggled with that because for most of my high school years I felt I was good at most everything I attempted.

And now I found myself in a foreign land, granted I did not have to learn a new language, but there are areas I served in where I literally could not understand a darn thing people were saying. To complicate matters, Elder Ricciardi was learning English on the fly himself. One time he wanted to "tactfully" tell me I had not done the best job in a discussion we had just taught. Here is how it was conveyed to me, "Elder Humphrey…how you say…the discussion was…let me think…what you say to them…how you say…very terrible…yes, thank you, you much very terrible." Sorry, but I was already down about how bad I was at missionary work, and on top of that his version of tactful feedback was "much very terrible"? I am sorry, I can only take so much abuse from the general public and now I have to hear broken English feedback? So, you can appreciate my constant avoidance of his "very much tactfully wonderful" observation and feedback (which is what we called it back then).

During the meeting with the couple we had just taught, I had totally messed up and made a very stupid and insensitive comment about the Catholic Church and the Church of England, so I knew his desire to give feedback was an undercover exercise to tell me that I left a very much terrible impression upon our investigators that night. So, I replied, "no, don't need to talk about the discussion, I felt great about it." He again tried to gently nudge me into a conversation as we got on our bikes. I took off like a rocket, I was in pretty good shape, and I felt that a good half mile distance would be the ticket. Forgetting he was Italian (they are bike riding maniacs) he caught up in no time and again attempted to give feedback. I became childish and started saying, "Sorry, can't hear you, I'm busy right now thinking about life." He finally stopped talking, and our bike ride to our flat (aka apartment) for the next 30 minutes was peaceful. When we finished companion prayers, I jumped in my bed and turned away from Ricciardi so he wouldn't attempt another feedback attack. He turned the light on and came over to the side of my bed to talk.

Thoughts on Caring Enough.

I warned him, "Elder Ricciardi, I don't want to talk about the discussion."

He said, 'I don't either.'

So, I sat up. "What do you want?" I said.

Ricciardi replied, 'I want nothing... but to ask you one quick question.' What he said next I was not expecting. He said, "Elder Humphrey, there are two reasons missionaries get along as a companionship. First reason when they are working together to be humble, obedient, and loving the people as a companionship. In other words, they are doing what is right together. However, the second reason missionaries will also get along is if they are both doing the wrong things together, as a companionship. Not getting up on time, not studying, breaking mission rules."

I remember thinking, "Where is the question in all this?'

Ricciardi then lowered his tone of voice and said, "I believe when missionaries do not get along, when they fight and argue, it is because one missionary wants to do what is right, and the other doesn't care." He then asked me the deadly question. "We do not get along Elder, so I ask you tonight. Please tell me which missionary you are, the one who wants to do right, or the one who does not care. Because if you believe that you are trying to do what is right, then I am the one choosing what is wrong, and I need to change so we can be one. Goodnight Elder."

I was floored. Normally that kind of talk from Ricciardi would set me off into a rage, but I felt the Spirit. In fact, I laid there, and tears came to my eyes. I had mocked

Ricciardi for so many of his methods. Here are some examples. Whenever we reached a neighborhood, he would pull out the street map and we would pray right there in the middle of the street for guidance. I thought that was silly. Sometimes he would stop our bike ride to a previously designated neighborhood and pray, right there in traffic with people staring at us. He would ask the Lord, "Are we going to the right neighborhood?" Then we would turn around to another destination and I would be so mad about backtracking 4 miles. I found these and many of his other habits so annoying and over the top. But I knew that night, that the answer to his question was that I was the missionary not caring enough.

That conversation actually transformed me as a companion, because I was embarrassed that I had been so disrespectful to him. In the deepest part of my heart, I knew he truly meant well in all his endeavors. I resented his spirituality and boldness because I was not sufficiently humble to acknowledge that I was nowhere near this guy in the spirituality department. Not close in terms of dedication, or his love for the people of England. Big moment for me. Very big. I woke up the next morning and became kind and stopped making what was already hard work so much harder for a companion who cared so much. I wanted us to get along for the right reasons. You know what? I almost immediately became happier. The work was still hard, the disappointment still came, but I stopped fighting Elder Ricciardi, and I began to feel myself becoming better.

The Sources of All Fear.

You know, there were days even when I was out with 18 months that I would wake up in the morning and not feel like talking to people. You would think a seasoned, veteran missionary 18 months under his belt would have conquered the fear by now. Satan never gives up trying to discourage missionaries from getting out and seeing the people. That is what a mission is all about, seeing the people. The adversary's greatest tool is fear. The greatest killer of missionaries is fear. It is important that you know as a fact, that fear is not a tool of God or his Son Jesus Christ. It is a tool of the devil, and Satan alone. Become self-aware as a missionary. You must be able to self-diagnose that when feelings of fear arise, you are being played by the devil.

I remember about a week after arriving in England Elder Ricciardi took me into the town center of Loughborough to street contact. We would split up (obviously still within eye contact of each other) and stop people in the open air malls downtown. I was absolutely terrified. I at least enjoyed the fact that when knocking doors some people would not answer the door, or not be home. But in the town center there was no way out. People were everywhere, and I was to stop them.

Two hours went by and I hadn't stopped anyone. I had given half-hearted attempts, but nothing had come of it and I was becoming depressed and discouraged. Elder Ricciardi noticed this and came over to me. "Let's take a walk", he said, and we left the town center.

Elder Ricciardi, forgetting we were not in Italy (where it is common for two grown men to hold hands in a show of friendship) grabbed my hand. There we were, walking to the local park holding hands. England is a liberal enough place that no one thought twice about it. When we got to the park we sat on a bench and Ricciardi asked me a question, "Elder, do you know who you are?" I thought this was one of those typical Sunday school questions, so I gave the typical answer, "child of God.' He laughed and opened his Book of Mormon to 3Nephi 5:13, "Behold, I am a disciple of Jesus Christ, the Son of God. I have been called of him to declare his word among his people, that they might have everlasting life."

After I read the verse, he turned to me and said, "You are a disciple of Christ! You have been called to declare his word to his people! Elder, you fear no man!" Something about those words got me pumped up! I literally felt the fear melt away. In fact, I actually decided to say the words myself, "I fear no man!" with a fist pump to boot. We marched back into town to continue the street contacting (didn't need to hold hands on the way back). I stood next to the entrance of a health club and committed myself to stop the next person to walk out. In no time at all, the fear that had paralyzed me came right back. I stood there and let the next five or six people pass by while my battle with Satan resumed.

In the Church we always comment on Laman and Lemuel and their wickedness. We view them as so opposite to Nephi, who is so strong, muscular (at least in The Book of Mormon pictures he is), tanned, bold, fearless. What we don't remember is that even though Laman and Lemuel saw angels, were even smitten by angels, it did not take them long to forget the miracles and go right back to their old doubting selves. I actually have some sympathy for them, in the sense that here I was fresh off a powerful spiritual boost from Elder Ricciardi, and for about 10 minutes I was right back in the epicenter of fear. But I recognized it and convinced myself that I must break this grip even at the risk of saying something stupid. Finally, I stopped a big brawny body builder. I stumbled through my dialogue and sounded like an absolute rookie, and then he responded to my fumbling with a shocking, "Yes" to the invitation to share a discussion with him. His name was Steve Gligoriavich and he was from Yugoslavia. He accepted the gospel over the next three weeks. Baptizing him was fun, because his huge frame made a splash that got some people in the first row wet. When the curtains to the font closed, he also did a no, no by sitting in the font like a hot tub and asked if he could just hang out for a while to take it all in. I told him, "Sure." The only thing waiting on the other side of that curtain was a bunch of his friends and church members, and oh by the way, the gift of the Holy Ghost. He got right out.

Street Meetings.

Elder Ricciardi was fond of street meetings in the town center. Every so often we would set up shop in the town center at a corner known for public preaching. The Mission President had mandated that no street meetings be held by missionaries due to the Bible bashing it promoted. That did not stop Elder Ricciardi. I never participated because I was A) too scared and B) felt it was so embarrassing to watch, let alone participate. One day while traveling to a town on the fringe of our area, we waited at a packed bus stop in a town called Barrow Upon Soar.

I said, "Elder Ricciardi, why do you hold those street meetings, I feel they are embarrassing and that we are making fools of ourselves." No sooner had I finished sharing my thoughts, than he stood up on a nearby vacant bench and introduced himself to the crowd of 60 or so waiting for buses. "We are missionaries from the Church of Jesus Christ of Latter-day Saints...." We did well that day handing out copies of the Book of Mormon. No one got baptized (that we know of), but we did teach some discussions. He stood up on that bench to do the very thing I was criticizing him for, to reinforce the fact that our challenge as missionaries for two years is simple, we are to see people, and when we are not seeing people, we are to try to see people. After the bus stop incident, I never again complained about street meetings, knowing full well the mere mention would send him to the nearest group of bystanders, even if it was just to prove to me that to preach is to stare what we fear most right in the face. Ricciardi once said, "If you want to punch Satan in the mouth, open your mouth and preach."

"The Field is White..." (keeping commitments).

One day while door knocking, we met the most amazing Scottish couple in the town of Loughborough. They were golden, which was a missionary term for if there was a font in the backyard this was happening now. No resistance at the door. Ricciardi didn't have to kick the door in with his usual tactics. We told them we had a message about the gospel of Jesus Christ we wanted to teach them. They said, "We love Jesus, please share it with us." Honestly, after all the door to door abuse I had taken for as long as I had been in England, I almost wanted to cry as this cute couple in their late 20s with two darling little girls just beamed. At one point while I was teaching about Joseph Smith, I felt the Spirit so strongly that I very unconventionally blurted out, "This feels so good I want to cry." And I did cry. They smiled, and even said that they had been looking for a church to join in the area since they had moved to Loughborough from Edinburgh, Scotland.

We came back for the second discussion, committed them to a baptismal date, and completed the other four discussions. Unfortunately, three or four baptismal dates came and went over the next two months. So, on one visit to their home Elder Ricciardi shocked me once again with his utter boldness. He said to the husband, "We love you, but you are not keeping any commitments which we give you. We are grateful you continue to see us, listen to our lessons, but I am convinced that you simply like just having us around. The problem is we cannot hang around. There is too much work to do in finding the Lord's elect, because they hear his voice and follow him."

The husband and wife looked confused, then upset, no doubt offended to essentially be called the un-elect by Elder Ricciardi. Not only were they uncomfortable, but I was now ready to wring my own companion's neck right in front of our investigators (I am not exaggerating). They went ahead and decided to not have any more visits and even gave the copy of The Book of Mormon back, which we insisted they keep. Then Ricciardi let them know how much we loved them, and that there was nothing to be offended by. They were not ready, and that was ok, because someday they will be, and when that day comes Ricciardi asked that they promise to at least hear the message again as many times as necessary for them to feel spiritually compelled to the ultimate show of commitment, baptism.

As we exited their home, right there on the street five feet from their porch, I angrily grabbed Ricciardi and told him he was surely going to hell for slamming shut the gate to baptism on this wonderful couple. We did not speak the remaining bike ride back to the flat.

The next morning in companion study Elder Ricciardi read the following scripture from D&C 4:4, "For behold the field is white already to harvest; and lo, he that thrusteth in his sickle with his might, the same layeth up in store that he perisheth not, but bringeth salvation to his soul."

Ricciardi said, "Elder, I know you're angry, but the scripture does not say the field is yellow ready to plant, brown ready to water, it says white, ready to harvest. We are harvesters Elder." I replied, "Ricciardi, D&C 18:10

106

says, 'Remember the worth of souls is great in the eyes of God.'" Every soul. His answer, as always, surprised me. "Elder Humphrey, it is the worth of souls that has you and me on missions in the first place. We could have spent all our time together with that golden family every day, making them feel good, them making us feel like we are getting missionary work done. The problem is, there are so many other souls ready to harvest, that it is our duty as missionaries to immediately move on to harvesting'. Not planting but harvesting."

"Were they a waste of our time?" I asked.

"Absolutely not Elder, because we have learned lessons about the importance of investigators keeping commitments that will bless us in our harvesting efforts going forward. They have learned the true gospel of Jesus Christ. Their time will come, but not with us as their teachers. We must move on."

Some major lessons came out of this experience with Ricciardi. I learned to put in a concentrated effort at helping our investigators keep commitments. There were times I thought Elder Ricciardi was way too hard on investigators about not reading when they had made a commitment to us that they would. When an investigator would say, "I was too busy."

I would simply say, "no problem; try to read before the next visit". Ricciardi despised the word try. After a particularly testy visit with investigators who I felt Ricciardi was too hard on for not reading, I rebuked him on the bike ride home. He asked me to explain why we give investigators commitments in the first place. I responded with many answers which he acknowledged were all sort of right. However, he wanted me to change my thinking about commitments.

He felt that commitments were given to investigators so that they could have opportunities to feel the Spirit when the missionaries are not around. He felt it was easy for investigators to feel good around two young clean cut, smart, religious persons like missionaries. It's easy to admire the sacrifice of young people who would give up 18 to 24 months in the prime of their youth. But the challenge comes in getting investigators to feel the Spirit in those private moments alone, reading marked passages, praying to the Lord, pondering the commitment to be baptized, giving up the coffee, asking the girlfriend/boyfriend to move out to adhere to laws of sexual purity, paying that first tithe. It is in these private moments that people realize when they do what they are asked, the feelings that come when the missionaries visit, and leaves when the missionaries leave, can actually continue to dwell with them, on their own, when the missionaries are not around.

Yearning for The Spirit.

A yearning to have this feeling all the time begins to swell within the investigator, and then the invitation to baptism becomes a natural progression rather than a nerve-racking request by the missionaries. This is why that golden family from Scotland I referred to earlier, at the end of the day never got baptized. They loved having us around. In my anxiousness as a new missionary I simply wanted to stay friends long enough for them to join the Church. Ricciardi was so right. When investigators keep commitments, especially the little commitments, they learn that the Spirit can be with them even when the missionaries are not around. That is when conversion occurs, then they walk into the font rather than being pushed.

When the investigator reads passages, prays on their own, ponders what they have been taught and are reading alone, their good feelings (the Spirit) move them from feeling obligated to the missionaries. They begin to ask themselves, "how can I have these feelings with me always?" It is a desire to keep those good feelings with them indefinitely. It is conversion by the Spirit, and not the personalities or admiration of the missionaries. Don't misunderstand, your personality and their admiration for your sacrifice opens the door, but the path of your investigator must be walked with a desire born of the Spirit. It begins with keeping those little commitments to read and pray. If we returned to an investigator's home to teach a second lesson and they had not read, we would read with them instead and postpone the lesson to next time. If they had not prayed, we would pray with them. The goal with commitments like these is that they must do it on their own.

Leaving on a Loving Note.

I must say in spite of what seemed like an uncomfortable end to our teaching of the golden family, Ricciardi always had a way of leaving people open to future opportunities. Occasionally we would be in the middle of a first discussion and you could tell the people we were teaching looked bored, not interested. Suddenly they would interrupt us, cut us off mid lesson saying, "Thank you, but we aren't interested". Most missionaries would want to try and salvage the situation, perhaps talk the investigator into becoming interested, you know, click into salesman mode. Not Ricciardi. He would close his scriptures, give a big Italian smile, and would ask for a favor. He would say, "Thank you for your time. If missionaries should come knocking on your door a week from now, a year from now, or twenty years from now, please let them in like you have allowed us. Because though the message will be the same, you will feel differently. Will you do that?"

A year after being with Ricciardi I was knocking doors in Nottingham, England when a man answered and we taught a family that let us in their home, because nine months earlier they had promised an Italian chap if any other Mormons came by they would let them in. Did we baptize this family in Nottingham? No. But when I left their home, I asked the same favor of them... again. Who knows by now how many other missionaries have entered homes that Ricciardi so kindly asked that favor of? When people reject the message, they are not rejecting you personally. Learn to shake off taking rejection so personally. Remember when I mentioned earlier that when rejected, Ricciardi gave that big smile? I always thought he was smiling to be polite before asking them to allow future missionaries to come again. He told me politeness was a small part of his big grin. The real reason for the big smile was gratitude that we could now move on to other fields that are white and ready to harvest. He loathed wasting time.

Facing Rejection.

Which brings me to this critical point. I can honestly say that one of the most valuable lessons I learned from Ricciardi was the importance of viewing rejection as positive. Yea sounds crazy huh? Take a minute and look through his eyes for a moment. He believed that when we were experiencing rejection, it was an opportunity to prove our commitment to the Lord. He felt that it was an opportunity to prove to the person rejecting our message that we are truly servants of the Lord. It's amazing the effect it has to smile at someone who is being rude to you, perhaps even yelling and cursing at you, making fun of you and then respond like Ricciardi and say, "Sorry to upset you, please have a nice day, if missionaries come by someday in the future please don't be mad, give them a chance." I would get angry during one of these confrontations and as a young don't know much missionary let my temper get the best of me and say, "You shut your mouth", or "Come out here and get me off your porch." (Sad to say I actually did say that once...or twice). To be honest, in my early, immature first few weeks, fighting back made me feel better. It didn't take long to realize that it would be a very long 2 years if I spent it telling mean people that they are ignorant and to shut up. When I would say to Ricciardi, "Why did you apologize to that jerk?"

He would say, "because it makes me feel happier." He understood that happiness is truly a choice, not a random event. He believed that rejection of any kind was a sure sign of the fact that God lives, and was an affirmation of the rightness of our mission.

One thing I remember vividly about Ricciardi was his ability to not let things get him down or upset. In fact, on the more difficult days, (and you know there are always plenty of those), he smiled and laughed more. On those particular days I found his extra dose of happy smiling Elder annoying. Yet again he would prove its value to me. He would say, "Elder Humphrey, I know we are in tune with the Lord, because He sent us to a neighborhood where no one wants to listen, and they are mean and confrontational. When I am prayerfully led to these kinds of situations, it confirms we are being led by the spirit because our Father knows how bad this neighborhood was going to be, and expected us to leave 20 houses ago. Yet here we are! This is awesome!!!" (By the way, Ricciardi's favorite American word was awesome). It was this kind of talk that led me to conclude that something was either not normal with my Italian compare (friendly way to call someone you know) or he was one of the three Nephites. After seeing how, and what he would eat, I eliminated the three Nephites theory.

When I was in high school, I worked at a golf course. I became friends with the assistant pro, and he started to give me free lessons. I quit after about 10 lessons for one simple reason. I was frustrated by the 55 things you have to think about almost simultaneously in order to have a good swing. The club pro finally advised me to stop taking lessons, go play and do one thing for him, just swing, swing, swing. That's it. Do not give any care as to where the ball goes, just swing. He told me, "Danny, you will enjoy golf better by just swinging." The same applies to missionary work.

Ricciardi saw the mission experience as incredibly simple. He understood that his mission was to speak to as many people as possible and that was it. Yes, there's a lot more to it than that, but a mission is nothing without talking. He would tell me, "Stop worrying about what you're saying, just open your mouth and say something." I took that advice to mean the Lord would always fill my mouth with exactly what to say. Truth is, I said some pretty stupid things, offended people many times (mostly accidental of course). But I began to enjoy missionary work when I concentrated on getting out the door and opening my mouth. Like the golf pro said, "Just go out and swing."

Getting the Elusive Second Appointment.

Ricciardi had this brilliant way of getting in the first discussion and committing new investigators to a second appointment. He would say, "If we took that family portrait on your wall and cut it into six pieces, and placed one piece in the frame, would you be able to comprehend the picture? Much like that one piece, we have given you one of six pieces, and for you to truly understand the restored gospel of Jesus Christ, we would like to give you the other five pieces and see what you think? Will you allow us to do this?" I actually found the more we loved the people of England and expressed that love to them, the bolder we could be without upsetting them.

Two Priests.

Ricciardi was very knowledgeable on the scriptures. I recall street contacting in the town center when I saw two Catholic priests across the courtyard walking up a ramp. I didn't want to have any conflict on this particular day, so I went to Elder Ricciardi and slyly suggested that we had spent ample time in the town center. He agreed and we began to put on our back packs. I was hoping we could leave before the priests noticed us or vice versa. It was while we began to ride out of the main mall area that Ricciardi spotted the two priests. He stuck his arm out to motion for me to stop. Ricciardi turned to me, let out a small Italian chuckle, and said in his thick Italian accent, "We must stay, Elder." As the priests approached us one of them said, "Ah the Mormons!"

Ricciardi responded, "That is correct!"

The priest said, "Out preaching about your Jesus today, eh?" Ricciardi responded, "He is your Jesus too, we do not want to monopolize him!"

The priests did not find his clever response humorous though I almost fell over with laughter. At that point I didn't even know Ricciardi had a sense of humor. The priests then turned into bashing mode and went on a spiritual tirade that lasted about 15 minutes. The whole time I was waiting for Ricciardi to unleash his scripture Bazooka. (His scriptures where legendary in our mission for being marked up for theological warfare). I did not know much about Ricciardi at this point in our companionship, but one thing I did know; he was powerfully knowledgeable on the scriptures and theological doctrines of other churches, with a particular fondness for Catholicism, which is the religion he was raised in. I had never seen him in action per se, and I was sure he was going to just dismantle their intellect with a tirade of his own. (For the record I discourage Bible bashing for its contentiousness, but I must say watching Ricciardi at work was a sight to behold).

To my surprise Ricciardi did nothing but listen intently. It frustrated me! "Come on" I thought, "They are winning for crying out loud!" Ricciardi just listened, occasionally nodding his head in acknowledgement of what they were saying. Then Ricciardi slightly tilted his head to me and out the side of his mouth whispered, "Watch this."

Suddenly Ricciardi raised his hand in front of the priests as a signal for them to stop talking, and in a deep voice said, "Can I ask you a question?" His sudden movement nearly startled them right out of their robes. He leaned forward into their faces and said, "Do you believe in the Holy Ghost?"

The priests answered, "You mean the Spirit of the Lord, the spirit of God, the Holy spirit? Of course, we do!"

Ricciardi replied, "That is good. May I ask you another question? Do you believe the Holy Ghost knows all truth?" The priests said. "Of course we do, we preach that in our own church, all Christians must believe the Holy Ghost knows all truth!"

Then Ricciardi replied, "That is good. Do you believe the Holy Ghost reveals truth to men?"

The priests came back with, "Yes! Do you think we are fools?"

Finally, Ricciardi asked, "Will you do me a favor?"

"What do you want?" they replied.

Then without warning Elder Ricciardi's voice took on a powerful tone that I had never heard him speak in before. I could have sworn he had a microphone in hand and that there was an echo to his words. "Please do two things before we come to visit you tomorrow at four o'clock. (That was the invite). I ask you to open your hearts and have a desire to know the truth, because if you have done these things before we come tomorrow, the Holy Ghost, the same Holy Ghost we have spoken of, will visit you and confirm unto you from within, the truthfulness of the message we will bring. I also want you to know that what you are feeling now is the Holy Ghost of which we have spoken!"

Tears filled my eyes as I stood there next to Elder Ricciardi. I pondered on how the power of the prophets of old caused people to quake, thinking those stories were relegated to a more ancient time and that things like that just don't happen anymore. I was wrong. The Spirit was present, and the priests looked really uncomfortable, "I thought holy cow, they are actually feeling the Spirit!"

The priests had a silent and uncomfortable reaction to Ricciardi's bold claim. Unwilling to admit what they were feeling (perhaps unable to define what it was) I contend to this day they know they felt something that spring day. The priests declined Elder Ricciardi's request and they promptly laughed at him as they immediately walked away. It was the kind of uncomfortable laugh you give when you are unsure of yourself and you simply want to get out of the situation.

In tears I turned to Elder Ricciardi and smiled. He laughed and said, "They felt the Spirit Elder, in high voltage!" We laughed and rode off, feeling like fearless servants of the Lord, called to preach his gospel to his people, that they might have everlasting life.

The day Ricciardi was transferred he admonished me to do as we had done that day in the park. "At any time should fear creep back into your heart, open the Book of Mormon to any page, read, and the book will remind you of who you are. Once you are reminded of who you are and what you have been called to and by whom, you will fear no man!" Many missionaries forget from day to day the power that has called them to this calling, which stands behind them every single day of the mission experience.

Measuring your Success as Obedience.

I learned many things from all my companions. Yet without a doubt Elder Ricciardi had the greatest influence on my mission. All my Ricciardi's experiences were not like the meeting with the catholic priests, much of his influence came in the little titbits of wisdom he would share, and without a doubt the hardest work ethic of any missionary I knew.

In my mission, statistics over the prior ten years (1976 to 1986) showed that the average missionary had 1.3 baptisms per year. In other words, the average missionary, after two years, would baptize 2.6 people by the conclusion of their mission. My district learned about this statistic the day before we left the MTC. I remember how disappointed I was at the prospect of spending two years to bring two and six tenths persons to the Lord's Church. Elder Ricciardi trained me when he was eight months out on his mission. Up to that point he had baptized over 60 people. He ended up leaving the mission with over one hundred baptisms. He would never talk about his baptisms. In fact, it was not until the end of my mission when I was working in the mission office that I had the opportunity to look up his extraordinary accomplishment.

One of the most challenging elements of the mission experience is how to judge whether you are a good missionary or not. It is baptisms? Is it number of lessons you teach? There are missions in the world where a missionary after two years experiences no baptisms. There are missionaries who find a family of 12 on their doorstep asking to be baptized (think South America).

The dilemma of new missionaries is to learn some way of gauging effectiveness and success. It is natural to use number of baptisms as the gauge of success. While number of baptisms is important, there is a far better more valuable gauge, obedience. I knew of missionaries in my mission who did not live mission rules, were not as committed as I think the Lord desired, yet they baptized. I really struggled with that because when I left the MTC it was my firm understanding that only obedient missionaries baptize. When I saw disobedient missionaries having baptisms, I began to con myself into thinking that getting up on time, reading scriptures, and other seemingly trite white bible rules didn't necessarily correlate with baptisms. I began to perceive that it would be easier to relax and baptize than to work so darn hard, be so disciplined and not baptize.

That "One Soul" is Yours.

Every missionary goes through a draught period in their mission life. A period of time where they are fighting homesickness, praying harder than they ever have, are living more righteously than ever in their lives up to this point in time, and no one seems interested in hearing the gospel. It is at this time that the Lord tests you as a missionary. The reason, I have always believed, is to see if you can be trusted. Father in Heaven has an incredible work to do to prepare the earth for the coming of the Lord Jesus Christ. The mission field has a dual purpose to bring souls unto Christ, and to sift us as missionaries into the parts we will play throughout our lifetime in building the Lord's kingdom, to prepare us for leading or prepare us for following, both are important, but what are followers without leaders? The missionaries who recognize the draught and remain strong to the higher law of missionary work (absolute obedience) end up converting the most critical investigator of all, themselves. You will be your greatest conversion in the mission field. In D&C 18: 15-16 it says,

"And if it so be that you should labor all your days in crying repentance unto this people, and *bring, save it be one soul* unto me, how great shall be your joy with him in the kingdom of my Father! And now, if your joy will be great with one soul that you have brought unto me into the kingdom of my Father, how great will be your joy if you should bring many souls unto me" (emphasis added).

I contend that the "one soul" is you. Imagine the insanity of sending 19 to 21 year old young people all over the world to be the ambassadors of something as critical as the restored Gospel of Jesus Christ. Frankly, it sounds crazy. But factor in a couple of things. Do most missionaries enter the mission field converted? I can only speak for me. I wasn't. I had good feelings about the Church, seminary, Joseph Smith, and the gospel, but converted? Not to the degree the Lord desires. That is the beauty of the mission experience. The Lord entrusts us to dispense his critically important message, knowing full well that in the process of delivering that message an unusual process occurs where the teacher of the message and the hearer of the message are both becoming converted at the same time. Not every hearer will be baptized, even though they feel the Spirit. Not every teacher will become converted. But here is what I do know. If you are absolutely obedient to the mission rules, you will become converted, and at that point you have accomplished what should be the greatest result of your missionary service. At the same time, you have the opportunity to bring others along the conversion path smack in the middle of your own conversion.

That is why mission success can only have one gauge, your personal conversion. This only comes from one attitude, that of absolute obedience. Baptisms happen or don't happen. Teaching opportunities can happen or don't happen. The blessings of the converted missionary last far beyond the mission experience. Learn this critical principle, all you need to do for two years is make sure that nothing but the truth comes out of your mouth to every single person you can possibly speak to (in golfing terms, just swing). Leave the conversion part to the Spirit, but your own conversion comes from that type of focus, baptisms or not. "How great shall be your joy when you bring save it be one soul" unto the Lord, and that soul is yours. That is the answer to what in my mind (and experience) constitutes a successful mission. Ricciardi did not let the statistics keep him from becoming a powerful missionary. But his effectiveness came from his own conversion to the Gospel of Jesus Christ in the mission field.

You will find that 80% of the missionaries do 20% of the work, and 20% of the missionaries do 80% of the work. It is unfortunate but true. That is why the greatest conversion that should take place in the mission field is your own! That is what is so incredible about missionary work, the closer you bring others to Christ, the closer you get to Christ yourself. I am not just talking about when you teach investigators and less actives, the missionary work you will do to help your companions come closer to Christ, and they for you, is a powerful work in and of itself, let alone the work to those who do not have the gospel. Ricciardi would say, "All you have to do is open your mouth Elder Humphrey, that's all." Ricciardi and I would challenge each other that once we walked out the apartment door, we would not let one person walk by without telling them who we are. I remember many mornings where we never left our street because there were so many people to stop. Ricciardi taught me to work smart. Every weekday at 3:30pm we stopped whatever we were doing and would never schedule appointments at that time of day. Why? Because we would go to the local elementary schools and greet parents as they were picking up their school children. In England, parents walk to school to pick up their kids. We would find a few families and walk them home as we discussed who we were and what we taught.

Make Time for Members.

Ricciardi must sound incredibly perfect to you. He had his weaknesses. He rarely worked with members. His sense of independence to a certain degree was a weakness (stubborn plus Italian is quite the combination). Ultimately, the members of the Church are the best way to bring people into the gospel as I am sure you already know. Truthfully, a lot of members were intimidated by Ricciardi's brash personality. Ricciardi always felt guilty when we were at member homes because cultivating member relations takes time, and he always felt like time was too precious. Hence, he saw member missionary work for the most part as a waste of precious time. Nevertheless, it is extremely difficult to be a good missionary without getting the members involved. Take the time to do that.

Lesson Learned.

One important experience I had, not with Ricciardi but because of Ricciardi, was a life changing event for me. After my first two months Elder Ricciardi transferred to another city. I spent the next two months with an elder who had three months left on his mission. To be candid, he was trunky, which back in the day was a term for ready to pack his trunk and go home. Our first morning together he woke up at 9am (I had companion study alone and watched him sleep for over 4 hours), we left the flat (apartment) and had breakfast at a local café (which in my first two months with Ricciardi we had never done because we were both too poor to spend any money) and we basically took a day off for my new senior companion to acclimate to his surroundings. At first, I felt relieved. It felt good to just relax. We got along great, laughed a lot. One P day we left our area boundaries to play golf (something Ricciardi would have considered a sin *and* it was against mission rules to leave your area without permission).

The days turned into weeks, and the weeks turned into a month. I started not sleeping well because I knew we were not doing the right thing. I was pressing this elder (who was the senior companion) about street contacting and going to the local schools in the afternoon. He just wanted to take it easy. We had long lunches, we hung out at members' homes, we changed P days on occasion to accommodate site seeing. By the end of our first month I felt sick. I realized that Ricciardi's influence, which I was so happy to get out from under, was now in me. I knew what the right thing to do was. Soon enough my senior companion and I began to not get along. We began fighting (not literally, but verbally).

One night after companion prayer, as we were going to bed, I went to his bedside and asked the elder why he thought we were not getting along. He said, "You are way too uptight Elder. Ricciardi must have brainwashed you or something." I told him that we got along initially because we were both relaxing together. But we were not getting along now because one of us wanted to work harder, and one of us didn't. I told him that if I was the one in the wrong to simply let me know. He agreed that we had essentially taken a month off. The next day our vigor for the work returned. I'm not trying to take credit here, but when transfer day came, I was transferred from Loughborough to Birmingham. This elder thanked me for being able to share my frustrations effectively. I had used Ricciardi's conversation word for word. Whenever you are not getting along with your companion, ask yourself, who of us wants to do right in this companionship? If you get along great with your companion, ask yourself, are we getting along for the wrong reasons (mutual lack of obedience, work ethic, dedication, spirituality) or for the right reasons?

Teaching with The Spirit

In D&C 50 verses 13-14; 17-22 it says, "Wherefore, I the Lord ask you this question—unto what were ye ordained? To preach my gospel by the Spirit, even the Comforter which was sent forth to teach the truth. Verily I say unto you, he that is ordained of me and sent forth to preach the word of truth by the Comforter, in the Spirit of truth, doth he preach it by the Spirit of truth or some other way? And if it be by some other way it is not of God. And again, he that receiveth the word of truth, doth he receiveth it by the Spirit of truth or some other way?

If it be some other way it is not of God.

Therefore, why is it that ye cannot understand and know, that he that *receiveth the word by the Spirit of truth receiveth it as it is preached by the Spirit of truth?" (Emphasis added)*.

22 Wherefore, he that preacheth (Missionary) and he that receiveth (investigator or companion), understand one another, and both are edified and rejoice together.

A few weeks into my companionship with Elder Ricciardi, I was ready to be the lead in teaching a discussion. I was nervous. We were teaching a family. The husband was a very articulate knowledgeable man. During the discussion, I really felt what I thought was the Spirit. I say thought because it is a big challenge for a missionary to decipher if you are actually feeling the Spirit, or if you just happened to be in a good mood. You know, you might have received a really awesome letter from home that morning, breakfast tasted especially good, your uncle sent extra money. Who knows the reason, but there is still personal doubt as a new/experienced missionary as to what would cause the kind of euphoric good feelings you might have while teaching someone the gospel. Anyhow, we reached a point in the discussion where I spoke about the First Vision. Deep emotion came over me as I recounted the story. Elder Ricciardi looked at me and I could tell he wanted me to identify the Spirit that was there in our discussion. Ricciardi was feeling it too. Again, doubts cropped into my mind, but I looked at the husband and said, "the Spirit is here with us, confirming the truthfulness of the things we are saying. How do you feel right now?"

He replied, "I feel fine, but I wouldn't go so far as to call it the spirit. You have a nice story to tell, it is interesting". I didn't know what to say, but Elder Ricciardi reliably stepped in. "Sir, that good feeling, as subtle as it may feel, is the Spirit, letting you know these things are true."

Again, the man was adamant that he certainly felt good, but would hardly call that the Spirit. Again, Ricciardi responded, "Sir, we feel the spirit, and as representatives of the Lord Jesus Christ, can assure you that this same Spirit is touching you now. We know this for one simple reason, we are telling you the truth, we feel the Spirit, and the Lord has told us in the scriptures that when the preacher preaches by the Spirit of truth and the hearer receives it by the spirit of truth, both are edified. In other words, because we are teaching you, we know if we feel the spirit, you feel it as well."

Again, the husband said, "Well, I also just had a cup of my favorite coffee, how do you know my good feelings aren't from that?"

Ricciardi replied, "Because there is no reason at this time, as we are teaching, for the Lord to only want to edify us at your expense of time and hospitality. We know that you feel it, you may not understand these feelings at this time, you might not even want to agree with us on this matter, but we know you are feeling the Spirit."

We were hastily asked to leave this man's home. He definitely did not take kindly to the suggestion that he did not want to admit to assigning his good feelings to the same thing we were. Here is why this is such an important story. Those verses above unveil a very powerful concept vital to missionary work. When you are teaching by the Spirit of truth, and you feel the spirit, know this, that the hearer of the message is feeling it too. Whether it is to the same magnitude as you or the same emotions is not relevant. Whatever extra good feeling they have, no matter how subtle, is the Lord's promised mechanism from the above referenced verses that, "…He that receiveth the word by the Spirit of truth receiveth it as it is preached by the Spirit of truth?"… "Wherefore, he that preacheth and he that receiveth, understand one another, and both are edified and rejoice together" (D&C 50: 19, 22).

Now that experience seems like we certainly did not rejoice together, but that was the investigator's choice, his freedom, if you will. Is this so? How are we to know? The truth is, the Spirit was there, he felt it, we felt it, we identified it, and he chose to assign those feelings to something else. That is ok. He has that agency. But we did what we were supposed to do, knowing that the promise of the verses from Doctrine and Covenants 50 indicate that if we feel it as the preachers of truth, the hearers are feeling it too. I testify to you that this is how missionary work gets done. Many will react as the man I just described. What you must come to terms with is that the Lord distributes his Spirit in these discussions, but it is still a world of agency. Did we understand one another in the way the verse above meant? Perhaps only in the sense that we made clear the Spirit was there and he made clear that his good feelings about our message doesn't necessarily mean it was the Spirit. Nevertheless, the Spirit was there, we felt it, and he felt it, and he kicked us out, and we knew we had done what the Lord wanted us to do (or should I say that Ricciardi did what the Lord wanted me to do).

Elder Ricciardi did not need him to agree with us to know that the Spirit touched him, because the Spirit touched us while we were teaching him the truth. If you will embrace these verses, open your mouth at all times in all places (just swing), be strictly obedient, your mission experience will change your life forever. These are courageous moments to boldly tell someone they are feeling something they don't either understand or necessarily agree with. But here is the key, many will rejoice together with you and many won't. You must be ready to make that bold statement when the spirit prompts, and not let fear (that tool of the devil and the devil alone) creep into your heart.

But if you don't follow the prompting, you are keeping investigators from the chance to understand that what they are feeling is directly correlated to the truth they are hearing. Remember, you teach truth and feel the Spirit, know that they are feeling the Spirit too. The difficulty comes in the courage to identify and explain it to the investigator, and the investigator's willingness to accept that this is what's happening. When you have meetings where the preacher (missionary) and hearer (anyone you are teaching, which includes your missionary companions) understand one another and rejoice together, it is life changing. Remember, this event still may not end in the investigator being baptized, but that does not take away from the courage to recognize and identify the Spirit when teaching gospel truths, and the effect that such experiences have on you personally.

You will not feel the Spirit in every discussion that you teach, I sure didn't. When you do feel the spirit, know that the spirit is not just touching you for your own personal edification and leaving everyone else in the discussion out in the cold. Heavenly Father can provide you those feelings of the spirit in your own private moments. While teaching investigators, he gives you those feelings to let you know that, "he that preacheth and he that heareth" are in the presence of the spirit of truth, who is there to confirm the words being spoken. Don't let an investigator who denies or chooses to not acknowledge the presence of the Holy Ghost make you lose confidence or else your future investigators will miss the opportunity to be taught the importance of what those feelings actually mean, and that those feelings come from God.

The wisdom of our God is epitomized in the missionary program of the Church. The Church asks young people to have a goal to be worthy to serve a mission. What the outside world sees as brainwashing, the Lord sees as striving for something so important that one would shun the vices of the world to not lose the privilege of serving a mission. Think of your life in 10 year increments starting from when you are baptized at 8 years old, from eight to 18, 18 to 28, 28 to 38, and 38 to 48 and on and on. What ten year segment contains the most life changing events? Answer: 18 to 28. So, the Lord understood the value of kicking off that critical time of your life with a mission. What better commitment for such an important period than to forget yourself for two years, delay formal education, and focus on God, Jesus, and everyone else but yourself. It is the perfect example of the classic scriptural saying to find yourself, you must lose yourself. You gain 10 years' worth of life experience from a mission. You leave at 19, 21 for the sisters, and return with ten years of life wisdom and experience crammed into 18 to 24 months. In that age segment of 18 to 28, not necessarily in this order, you serve a mission, get an education, marry, choose a profession/occupation, and have children. There is no other ten year increment with so much hanging in the balance. Wow, what a wise Heavenly Father to place the mission experience as the springboard for such a critical decade of life.

The Prayer Room

This last story runs very deep in my heart, as it represents a major turning point in my thinking about mission life. As I mentioned earlier, I was transferred to Birmingham as my second area. It was a tough blue-collar city, populated with a lot of people from all over the world. My new companion was an elder from California who had one month left on his mission. We were in a part of Birmingham known as Sparkhill. Tough neighborhood, with lots of people from Pakistan and India. Very Muslim influence, so you can imagine how missionaries preaching Christianity might feel surrounded by mosques. I remember on the second or third day wondering, "Why put missionaries amongst people who are so devoutly religious but don't care about Jesus Christ?" A month later my senior companion went home, and I received a new companion from Germany who also only had one month left on his mission. This was very difficult for me, as I wondered if God was punishing me. It was very emotional for me to have had two consecutive months of sending missionaries home. Muslim area, two companions, last month for each. Month three I received a new companion and I became a senior companion. My new companion absolutely didn't care about his mission, and was frankly biding his time, watching the clock, simply waiting to go home (and he had 14 months left).

I deployed the Ricciardi work schedule on him, and he began to come around. Two months later when he left, he thanked me, but he was really thanking Ricciardi. This was a tough area, we had taught very few discussions, handed out hardly any copies of the Book of Mormon, no investigators to church since I had arrived. It was wearing on me. At that point in time I was called to be a trainer. I thought, what a bummer to have to train a new missionary in such an armpit of the mission area (please excuse that reference). My spirits were really low, because I had been working harder than ever, being more prayerful than ever, really obedient, and no one wanted to hear our message. At that same time, I was seeing missionaries in neighboring parts of Birmingham scheduling baptisms. One companionship bragged that they had just come back from three days in Scotland (not just outside our area, outside our mission, which is an absolute no) on a site seeing outing and they had a baptism scheduled the next weekend. I couldn't believe it. That night I asked the Lord, flat out, "why do this to me? Why should I work so hard when those other Elders are having fun, being disobedient, and still baptizing?"

I believe this kind of pivotal moment comes into every missionary's time in the field. It is a moment where you have to decide what is more important, obedience *or* everything else. I was now praying to leave the city of Birmingham, because I'd had enough. When transfers came, I thought for sure I would leave (typically missionaries stayed in an area three to four months). I was now into month seven, but neither of us was transferred. Now I was really mad.

The next morning after the news of no transfer, I got up and went into a spare room on the third floor of our flat that I regularly used for personal prayer. I said what I would describe as an angry prayer. I asked the Lord what the use of staying so darn obedient was if I was to have no baptisms. I said, "Father, you are almighty, I pray over the map every day, I stop our bike rides at the slightest prompting to rethink what we are doing, where we are going, all to prove that I am listening, and you still send me to neighborhoods where there is nothing but vile, mean, personal rejection." Ricciardi of course would have been overjoyed at those kinds of prospects. I wasn't. I could write ten pages about what I said that morning in that damp, musty, moldy room.

Then it happened. The answer to prayer that changed the course of my mission and frankly my life. Let me fast forward a minute to May of 2007 before I finish the prayer room story. I was working in New York City, living in

New Canaan, CT (had lived there 14 years), and married with six children and one day I received a call from an old mission friend Michael Walker. We were never companions, but back in 1986 he and his companion at the time had moved in with me and my companion for three weeks while they looked for an apartment in another part of Birmingham.

He was coming to New York City on business and asked if we could meet for breakfast. I had not seen or heard from Michael in over six years, so I was surprised not only to hear from him, but that he sounded so anxious to see me. I wondered if he was ok or needed help. I picked him up from the airport that morning and we had breakfast at my favorite spot in Manhattan. We reminisced about a lot of mission memories, and then seriousness fell over our meal. He looked at me and said, "Can I ask you a question about something that happened when I was living with you and Elder DeGala in Birmingham?" The strangest impression came over me when he asked that because at the very moment, he asked the question I already knew what he was going to ask me. I knew this had to do with the prayer room.

I quietly said, "sure."

The first line out of his mouth was, "There was this room on the third floor of that apartment in Birmingham...' I immediately raised my hand motioning for him to stop talking and I began weeping so uncontrollably that restaurant patrons sitting around us became uncomfortable and uneasy. He waited for me to respond. It took ten minutes for me to gain my composure. He patiently waited, then continued, recounting to me that he had seen me pray in this moldy smelly room in our flat, and he had started using it for his own personal prayers. One morning he came to the room to pray and could hear me praying

130

out loud in the room. He left and came back ten minutes later and could still hear me praying. He returned several other times over the next hour intending to use the room for his own prayers and could still hear me in there praying. I had never until that day prayed out loud in my personal prayers, nor had I prayed for longer than 5 minutes, but that morning, with all my frustrations and anger, I decided to say my prayer out loud and I had plenty to say. My friend recounted that though he could not hear what I was saying, when he pressed his ear to the door he could sense the earnestness and emotion of my prayer.

He returned again and this time did not hear me praying, but below the door could still see my shadow. Another 20 minutes went by and upon hearing me open the door he came down the hall and saw my eyes almost swollen shut from crying. As we passed each other no words were exchanged. After telling me the story up to this point over breakfast, he began to weep, as he told me that he entered the room to pray and a flood of emotions enveloped him immediately without explanation, causing him to cry and wonder what had taken place in that room.

So there we were at breakfast 21 years later, in New York City, and he wanted to ask me a simple question, "What happened in that room?" That brings us to the moment that changed my mission forever. What happened in that room is simple. For the first time in my whole mission I asked through earnest prayer for answers I deeply desired and needed, and I received an answer from the Lord, a literal answer that I could hear with the same clarity and resonance that my friend was talking with during breakfast.

That morning I had prayed for close to 45 minutes when I decided to cease praying, still not having formally closed the prayer, just quiet in my thoughts and tears. I was having thoughts of going home, giving up. Then I heard this message: "Elder Humphrey, I am here. I know who you are. I sent you to those neighborhoods, the very ones where you experienced nothing but rejection. I prompted your changes in direction to even more difficult neighborhoods. I know where each of the elect in your area resides. I know their names. I could send you to those addresses only and save you the time and sacrifice looking for them. But Elder Humphrey, what good would that serve you? The mission experience is to do what you are told, when you are told, to go where you are asked, and know that the blessing comes from enduring what I ask of you. This is not about you; it is about opening your mouth at all times in all places. Doing my will without thought to the end result or consequence. This is what serving a mission is."

That day in September of 1986 completely changed my focus. My anger went away. I became cheerful again for the first time in many months. When doors slammed in our faces, I would say to my companions, "The Lord knows these doors are slamming in our faces. This is part of his plan, the experience. He sent us to this neighborhood; he needs to know we can be trusted servants. That we will actually go where he wants us to go, do what he wants us to do, when he wants us to do it." I became jovial. Missionary work became fun, not work at all, because I stopped taking the rejection so personally and blaming myself. I now knew that all I had to do was talk to as many people as I could for the remaining 14 months, make sure that only the truth came out of my mouth, be prayerful about everything, and the Lord would do the rest. The week before I was transferred out of Birmingham, we baptized a woman. Nearly 8 months in that area and we finally saw someone step into the waters of baptism. Patience and prayer saved me from possibly quitting.

C.S. Lewis, one of my favorite authors, said something that to me captures what it means to see the Lord Jesus Christ while on your mission. He said, "We can say we believe in Christ as we believe in the sun at noon day, not that we can see it, but that by it, we can see everything else." (*C.S. Lewis, Is Theology Poetry?*) The things you will witness on your mission, is what makes you a witness of the Lord Jesus Christ. By no means am I suggesting you are a witness in the way that our apostles and prophets are, I am saying that to see people change their lives, to love people from another place, is a testament to the existence of God and His son Jesus Christ. Even as I write this, I am looking out my kitchen window, I see the trees swaying, I see grass and flowers, but I don't see the sun. However, it is the light of the sun that allows me to see what I see, and that is how I know the sun exists. The existence of the Son of God has that same value to us, as C.S. Lewis put so well, it is because we can see at all that we know Christ lives.

Thank you for the opportunity to share some thoughts. I have a deep abiding passion about missionary work. I know that your family does too because I have seen it. I will never forget the unconquerable spirit I became on my mission. To walk off that plane and know that I gave it my all was a powerful testament to me that God lives. As you know, you cannot fake or feign a mission. I have over my post mission years attended many missionary homecomings. It's not hard to tell who really gave themselves to the work, and who had a two year somewhat interesting experience. Going on a mission, and serving a mission are two different things. Most anyone can go on a mission, but serving a mission is a whole other ballgame. It is in your blood and upbringing to be nothing but the best missionary. Give Satan a good strong kick in the mouth and just swing. Thank you for your service to the Lord.

Vaughn J. Featherstone said it best and his poems are attached separately. (See attached Poems).

Keep up the good work,

Love,

Danny Q. Humphrey


## POEMS BY VAUGHN J. FEATHERSTONE

The Champion

The average runner runs until
The breath in him is gone,
But the champion has the iron will
That makes him carry on.

For rest the average runner begs
When limp his muscles grow,
But the champion runs on leaden legs.
His courage makes him go.

The average man's complacent when
He's done his best to score,
But the champion does his best and then
He does a little more.


You Can Do Anything You Must Do


If you want a thing bad enough

134

To go out and fight for it,

Work day and night for it,

Give up your peace, and your sleep and your time for it;

If only your desire,

Makes your aim higher

Never to tire of it,

If life seems all empty and useless without it

And all that you dream and you scheme is about it,

If gladly you'll sweat for it,

Fret for it,

Pray with all your strength for it,

If you'll only go after the thing that you want,

With all your capacity,

Strength and sagacity,

Faith, hope, and confidence; stern pertinacity,

If neither poverty, nor pain, or famished and gaunt,

Nor sickness or pain,

to body or brain,

Can turn you away from the Aim that you want,

If dogged and grim you besiege and beset it,

You'll get it.

Printed in Great Britain
by Amazon